JOURNAL FOR MARY

JOURNAL FOR MARY

By

SISTER M. MARGUERITE ANDREW, RSM

THE CHRISTOPHER PUBLISHING HOUSE
BOSTON, U.S.A.

DEDICATED

with love

to

The Honorable Judge and Mrs. E. D. E. Rollins

with a prayer that they may go through Mary

to Jesus

TABLE OF CONTENTS

AUTHOR'S NOTE

In the Journal itself I have not attempted to document formally the information given. I have used freely:

The Catholic Encyclopedia
The Roman Missal (Especially for the *Missae pro Aliquibus Locis*) published by Benziger Brothers, New York, 1956
H. M. Gillette's *Famous Shrines of our Lady*, The Carroll Press, Westminster, Maryland, 1950
Zsolt Aradi's *Shrines to Our Lady Around the World*, Farrar, Straus & Young, Boston, 1954
Maus' *The World's Great Madonnas*, Harper & Bros., New York, 1947
Archbishop Finbar Ryan's *Our Lady of Fatima*, Browne & Nolan, Ltd., Dublin, 1943

But the information gleaned from these books could have been obtained from many other sources as well; in any place where I have quoted verbatim, I have given credit, except in the case of the Bible (usually the Douay version); and here, where the quotations have been so familiar for so many years and in so many publications, I have not clogged the script with references.

In the more formal parts of the book, which are articles that have been published in various magazines, I have given sources in proper order.

9

Many of these articles, stories, and poems have appeared before in:

The Catholic Educator (or Journal of Religious Instruction)
The Catholic Miss
Fatima Findings
The Messenger of the Sacred Heart
The Rosary Magazine
The Sentinel of the Blessed Sacrament
The Voice of St. Jude

Permission to reprint is gratefully acknowledged.

JOURNAL FOR MARY

OUR LADY OF LITERATURE

Sweet Lady, teach me, let me learn the art
    You knew in Bethlehem,
When many words you kept within your heart
    And pondered over them.

My songs are harsh, the stress and rhythm wrong,
    And hesitant the chord;
One song you sang your whole life long
    And magnified the Lord.

My words lie in the rough-hewn ore
    In stubborn stiffness furled,
One shining Word sheathed in your heart you bore,
    And gave to all the world.

Seven words you heard beneath a bleeding cross
    Were traced in epic pain
Before you faced the agonizing loss
    That meant your children's gain.

Sweet Mother, teach me, let me learn the art
    You knew on Calvary;
The broken Word you pressed against your heart
    Was Love and Poetry.

Journal for Mary

I

1. SEPTEMBER

My Mother, I begin this Record for you in the very appropriate month of September. It is appropriate for a number of reasons. We celebrate your birth on the eighth, your holy name on the twelfth, and the twenty-fourth is your feast under the name of Our Lady of Ransom but we call it our own as that of Our Lady of Mercy.

There are so many things to be said *to* you, Mary, as well as to be said *of* you. I have no doubt that no new thing can be said of you, but all that can be said is re-newed year after year and century after century. It's all re-said in a fresher, different way so that it appeals to the current reader of each generation. For example, comparatively few persons of today would go back to the writings of Origen, St. Jerome, St. Augustine, or St. Basil; but many writers, learned and skilled in research, would go back to them and reproduce their wisdom and authority for the readers of today. In fact, when one scans the shelves of the convent library (each book with its copious bibliography), one wonders what new thing could possibly be said of you, what new aspect could possibly be presented. To take one instance: there is quoted as a source Bourasse's, "Summa aurea de laudibus Beatae Mariae Virginis, omnia complectans quae de gloriosa Virgine Deipara reperiuntur" (13 volumes, Paris, 1866)!

What St. John said of Our Lord: "If everything that Jesus did and said were written, the world would not contain all the books" must surely apply to you in another way. But as for the things that can be said *to* you: they are varied and as multiple as all the leaves of all the trees. You see, Mary, there is a little prayer that goes something like this: "Sweet Mother, I am thine; keep me as thy property and possession." But each individual who is proud to be known as your "property and possession" would have much to say to you in his own individual way, though still saying with the Psalmist:

"My heart overflows with a goodly theme as I sing my ode to the king. My tongue is nimble as the pen of a skillful writer."

Someone asked if I was undertaking this Journal because of special devotion to you, my Mother. Yes — and no. I was not always so especially devoted to you. I went my way in careless childhood, devout, yes — but looking back with the maturity of age I think most of my devotion consisted in enjoyment of the stale odor of incense in an empty church, of the sunlight shining through the reds and blues and purples of the stained-glass windows, of the majesty and melody of High Mass, of the dreams and images which the eloquence of a sermon superinduced — as well as of the sensible feeling of consolation with which your Son nourished me in those early years.

Then. Then came a time when I had a precarious toe-hold on the edge of an abyss; and, desperately, to keep balance, to avoid the sight of the terrifying depth, I wrenched myself back and turned; and there — there you were, filling my whole horizon. I knew you then as the Refuge of sinners, the Comforter of the afflicted. Yes, you have filled my whole horizon ever since.

I say this, though, with a sense of utter diffidence. We had once in our school, Mary, a girl who was so devoted to you. She was President of the Sodality, she wrote articles about you. After graduation, she came back and addressed the Sodality on devotion to you, telling how in the morning she offered every step, every act to Jesus through your Immaculate Heart. But now — she has married out of the church, married a notorious philanderer, and this her second husband-so-called boasts that she, his fifth wife, has more glamor than all the other four put together. O Mary, pray for her! Poor human nature — there are no depths to which we may not fall; there are no heights to which we may not aspire provided we do not lose our "savor" — that is the individuality of our own particular method of carrying out our Father's will.

That reference of our Lord's to salt losing its savor: sweet Mother, I think perhaps that is the possible explanation (oh, I tread lightly, tread lightly here) of the importance that God the Father attaches to our free will. He *wants* people to act according to the temperaments, skills, inclinations, traits both physical and mental with which He has endowed them. Like ourselves, when we "create" a thing: if we whittle a top that is supposed to spin a certain length of time, or in a certain direction, we watch it with delight, not only because we made it, but also because it will go off on its own toppish sort of way, and much as we can predict the results, we still are interested in watching it. Herein is the wisdom of the Little Flower, comparing herself to a toy.

"If the salt lose its flavor, wherewith shall it be salted?" That is, if you don't act according to the temperament, characteristics, and capacities that make up your own individuality, what good are you? What good is a poor and bound-to-fail imitation of somebody else? There, too, is the possible interpretation of your Son's terrible words in describing hell: Everyone shall be salted with fire — every victim shall be tormented by the very traits that would have redounded to his glory and reward had they been properly used.

Sweet Mother, intercede for sinners! Intercede for those who know not and love not your Son! Save them from hell while there is yet time. Save from hell those poor victims of Soviet tyranny who are being too brutalized to know right from wrong! They are, as it were, being deprived of their own personality to serve a Godless, man-made creation called "The State," or "The People."

It would be simple, Mary, to explain about personality in terms of heredity, environment, and influence; but just here there comes in that intangible, unpredictable, unchartable something, so that the equation might read: heredity (but just such and such elements in heredity) plus environment (but not every detail therein) plus influence (but only that portion of it that is yielded to, whether consciously or unconsciously) plus X equals you. Only there is no possible finite way of giving any clue to the evaluation or concrete worth of that "X."

Come to think of it, Mary, it's easier to explain that X-ness in you than the X-ness that goes to make up the me that is me; and that is why I want to talk about you rather than me — the only thing is that the past, present, and future in terms of your history are inextricably mixed with mine. Rumer Godden has a lovely book, the title of which I envy: *Take Three Tenses.* I always want to take three tenses. I want to carry along with me all the worth-while past that leads up to the lovely, sacred, all-too-fleeting present, and carry both along into a future exciting with its possibilities, secure in its confidence that the will of Divine Providence will arrange all things sweetly. I realize that the desire to have all three tenses at once is a reflection — faint but reliable — of the satisfaction of Eternity, when we shall arrive at the all-embracing, ecstatic NOW.

What a past you carried along with you, Mother! There was the earliest prophecy of you: Even when God in His anger was berating Adam and Eve, while the angel was standing by waiting with the flaming sword to bar the entrance to Eden; even then, it seemed, He could not hide His bountiful mercy, and mingled His reproaches as it were with the words horrendous to Satan, but comforting to the victims of his deceit:

"She shall crush thy head and thou shalt lie in wait for her heel."

Thus the devil was condemned to lie in quivering, fearsome questionings as to *how* that should be. What greater punishment than to be made to cower under a threat of a mysterious, inexorable future punishment?

Here, Mary, is not only a threat to Satan, but also a forecast of one aspect of your character; you are to be a woman fearless enough to crush with your unflinching heel whatever danger lurks in your pathway however much your woman's fastidious delicacy might shrink from what is repulsive.

Then there was that promise made to Achaz — a promise was almost lost when stubborn Achaz, in spite

of being urged by the Highest Authority to ask for a
sign, replied in his self-righteousness: "I will not ask,
I will not tempt the Lord." The Lord God must have
felt like saying to him: "Here, you foolish creature,
there are plenty of people who ask for signs when they
have no right to ask for them; why don't you take advantage of the opportunity I'm giving you?" And what
an opportunity! There were to be no limits: "either in
the heaven above or the depth of hell." But instead of
withdrawing His offer, our God answered tolerantly:

"All right; then I Myself will give you a sign that you
would never have dreamed up for yourself: a virgin
shall conceive and bear a son."

That is not all. The Lord God continues almost as
though ruminating His plans within His own divine
counsel: "His name shall be called Emmanuel — God
with us." That mysterious diet is prescribed: "He shall
eat butter and honey." Why? "In order that he may
know to refuse evil and choose good." Butter and
honey: the richness of God's providing, the sweetness
of His dispensation. But it would be as Jeremias is to
say later:

"The Lord will not turn away the wrath of His indignation till He have executed and performed the thought
of His heart. In the latter days, you shall *understand*
these things."

Again, in the long past that leads to you, Mary, there
is foretold the very city in which it shall take place that
"a woman shall encompass a man — a virgin shall bear
a son." Poor Bethlehem! It's a wonder that our Lord
Christ did not include it in His reproaches to Jerusalem,
to Capharnaum, to those other cities where He dwelt
and taught: "If thou hadst known in this thy time of
visitation the things that are to thy peace!"

There are many references in the Old Testament, Mary, that can be (and have been) applied to you: the blossoming almond tree, for instance, or that cloud "no bigger than a man's hand at first." I feel that these inspired words are made according to the individual understanding of each prophet. Perhaps the sacred writer was particularly interested in clouds, or blossoming almonds (or rods), or whatever he wrote about, without knowing that it referred to you. Undoubtedly he was deeply, poignantly interested in the coming of the Redeemer; but it may be that he did not realize the connection between his God-dictated words and the woman that was to be you, my Mother. Surely he didn't, or he would have broken forth into ecstatic recognition of the connection. Each wrote as he knew how according to his personality: that was the "flavor" of his salt.

I mentioned clouds, sweet Mary, and then realized that there is such a variety of symbolism for you in this particular nature-item — a symbolism that has not been made much of: When Moses had gone up to the Mount, a bright cloud overshadowed him; God called to him from the midst of the cloud. The cloud covered the tabernacle: the Lord came down in a cloud and spoke. A little cloud rose up from the seas. God promised that he would dwell in a cloud. He spread a cloud for his people's protection. "My throne is in a pillar of cloud" . . . as a cloud of dew in the day of harvest . . . your mercy is as a morning cloud . . . These references are intriguing, O my Mother, and it's a wonder someone has not come up with the title "Our Lady, pillar of cloud" or something like that.

But Mary! Of all the forecasts of your coming, the most poetic is that passage on wisdom that is always applied to you: "The Lord possessed me in the beginning of his ways . . . the depths were not as yet and I was already conceived . . . when he prepared the heavens I was present . . . I was with him, forming all things and was delighted every day, playing before him at all times . . . playing in the world, and my delights were to be with the children of men."

How the angels must have rejoiced in your birth! How tantalizingly few details are authentically brought down to us! The names of your parents we know from tradition: Joachim and Ann. It is also a tradition that they were old when you were born, and perhaps that is why they presented you to the Temple at such an early age. Whether you had brothers and sisters has never been definitively taught: certainly our Lord had many cousins — He chose four of them for His Apostles.

And where were you born? Some of the Fathers say Sephoris, a little town about three miles north of Bethlehem; some say, surprisingly, in Bethlehem itself — that certainly would justify the known fact that Joseph and you had to go back there to register for the census. A third supposition is that Jerusalem was your birthplace. Many take it for granted that you were born in Nazareth. All these traditions are sacred and, because much learned research has gone into each supposition, they are not to be discounted lightly. But for us — what real difference does it make?

We have you here and now in our daily lives, and we pray daily that you pray for us at the hour of our death. That's why those three tenses are important: the forecast of your birth, the actual facts of place and time and parentage, and the future for you and for us, O Mary, especially at the end of life. But the interests are here and now: Methods have changed — St. Ann may not have had the assistance of a midwife, certainly not of a doctor. Your coming may have been such a natural, effortless one that she needed no assistance, like the birth of Jesus from your womb, my Mother. Certainly it is to be taken for granted that St. Ann, in her pregnancy, did not have a monthly check-up for weight and diet and so on. Quite likely she did not prepare a layette and bathinette for you, and all the frilly fussy things that babies have these days. But oh! If only St. Ann or St. Joachim or *somebody* had kept a "baby record" or a journal of your early days! Your first word, your first step. Your genealogy yes — that was crucially important, but if only somebody had written in all the homely appealing little details instead of all those "begats." It has been suggested, Mary, that all the names mentioned in that genealogy are those you meant to "forget" — because you are the Woman of the new dispensation.

Well, since no homely details have come down to us, then we can only celebrate your birthday according to our own devotion, plus the liturgy, tradition, and inspired writings that we have. And in my case, I assume that no poem proclaiming the jubilation of nature at your birth, no vision or revelation (such as those of Mary of Agreda or Catherine Emmerich, worthy though they may be of reverence) can really do justice to the momentousness of the event. Therefore, in my heart I chant the lovely poems that tell of nature doing homage to you, I read with admiration the accounts of you (whether divinely or humanly inspired) and I greet you in my own way, Mary, according to the individual "flavor" of my "salt" and say: "Happy Birthday!"

This, the eighth, is the day our postulants enter,

Mary, and they are always too few. After supper —
their first day in the convent, they will kneel at your
altar and recite the "Act of Oblation and Consecration
to the Most Blessed Mother of God." The words, in
their sonorous phrases and involved sentences, Mary,
will mean more to them as their "Mary life" goes on.

Personally, I have so many reasons for being glad
of your birth. My human mother's name was yours,
and how she loved it: Mary Regina. One of her daughters has that queenly name: Elizabeth Regina. Two
of her children were born at the time the Angelus was
ringing, so she called one "Marie Angela," and the
other, born on your very own birthday, "Alma Estelle."
As for me, sweet Mother, I've entered a religious con-
gregation dedicated to you, and at my reception of the
habit, I, like all our members, was given the name of
Mary as well as that of a special patron saint.

So, Mother of God, with my own particular "salti-
ness" I am beginning this journal for you in your own
particular month, a month of many of your other feasts:
the twelfth, that of your holy name which has been
translated into so many forms and has been interpreted
with so many meanings: Miriam in Hebrew, Maryam
in Syriac, Maria in Latin, Marie in French. Besides
our own form "Mary" we have so many affectionate
derivatives: Marietta, Marina, Marita, May, Myra, etc.
The meaning of your name? "Bitter" according to one
authority (because of your sorrows, Mary?) or according to others: the healed one, the well-nourished one,
the ruling one, the gracious or charming one, the
exalted one; lastly: the beautiful and therefore the
Perfect One.

On the fifteenth, we have what seems a contradiction: your *feast* of sorrows. I count so many more than seven, Mary, but of course that's because many of your sorrows are derived from the major ones. But then, too, I count for each sorrow a counterpart of joy: there was no room for you in the inn, but the stable enabled you to receive the adoration of the shepherds in privacy. Your Son was circumcised, but it was a moment of joy when He was given His Sacred Name. You must have sorrowed over the slaughter of the Innocents — even while you rejoiced in the safety of Egypt and the protection of St. Joseph. Jesus' loss in the Temple meant the corresponding joy of finding Him. And so it goes all through, until, in the end: His death meant the beginning of life for your children.

Our Lady of LaSalette, we greet you on the nineteenth. Your appearance at LaSalette must have been a disappointment to you, sweet Mother — speaking humanly that is. Melanie and Maximin were so ordinary, mediocre, and while that doesn't prove anything since it's obscure characters you like to appear to — the remarkable thing is they continued to be ordinary and mediocre (so far as we know) even after your visits. Perhaps it's wrong to think it might be a disappointment, though, for you accomplished your mission in combating blasphemy, the disregard of Sunday, the mockery of Religion. Apart from the other details of their lives, it can be truly said that Melanie and Maximin did your bidding courageously and faithfully. And there were the usual results: the spring of water, the cures, the magnificent basilica, the continuation of devotion and pilgrimages to you under this title — and the message so successfully proclaimed:

"Unless people repent and do penance, the world shall perish."

On the twenty-fourth we celebrate your feast of Mercy "with joy and devotion."

My Mother of Mercy, you can say to us and to all the world (and much more truly) the words that Job said in his affliction:

"I delivered the poor man that cried out; and the fatherless that had no helper. The blessing of him that was ready to perish came upon me, and I comforted the heart of the widow . . . I was an eye to the blind and a foot to the lame . . . and the cause which I knew not, I searched out most diligently."

Make this true of us, your children, too, won't you, Mary? Let us seek out most diligently the "cause," the cases that need our ministration, as well as minister to those who come to us for help!

Our Lady, helper of the poor, sweet Mother celebrated under so many titles, I have written the article that follows to explain all this in a more formal style.

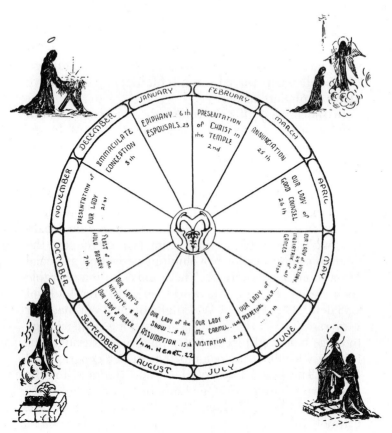

OUR LADY OF MANY FEASTS

2. OUR LADY OF MANY FEASTS

Holy Mother Church does not leave us long without a liturgical feast of Mary. Indeed, it would seem that Our Lady herself has seen to it that her children (especially her missal-using children) should have many reminders of her.

In the liturgy all year-round there is not a month without a special feast for her — all classes of feasts, from doubles of the first class down to the simple feasts, and then to those that are celebrated by special grant only in certain localities.

One device of Our Lady's to keep us ever mindful of her is to give us what we might call geographical feasts. She appears in certain places, or favors certain localities with great graces and miracles; thereupon the Church establishes for her children's devotion a special Mass in commemoration. There must be innumerable such shrines all over the world, such as Our Lady of LaSalette, Our Lady of Walsingham, etc. We may but very rarely have the privilege of making a pilgrimage to those hallowed places, but a pilgrimage through our missals will allow us to honor her in her geographical feasts. The best known of these and the ones for the Universal Church are: Our Lady of Lourdes, February 11; Our Lady of Fatima, May 13; Our Lady of Mt. Carmel, July 16, and Our Lady of Loretto, December 10. The Collects in the Masses for these feasts show the significance of honoring the places honored by Our Lady. For example, the Collect for December 10 pleads:

"God, who in thy mercy didst sanctify the Blessed Virgin's house . . . and didst miraculously place it in the heart of Christendom, grant that we may shun the abodes of sinners and become worthy to dwell in thy own holy house."[1]

Then there are Our Lady's historical feasts — that is, those commemorating some event in her life; there are ten of these: her Immaculate Conception, December 8; her birthday, September 8; her Presentation in the Temple, November 21; her betrothal to St. Joseph, January 23; the Annunciation, March 25; her visit to Elizabeth, July 2; her Expectation of the birth of Christ, December 18; His birth, December 25; His presentation and her own purification in the Temple, February 2; and lastly, the glorious consummation of her earthly life: the Assumption of her body to Heaven, August 15. There have been many books written, purporting to be the life of Mary, but outside of the meager account of her that we have in Holy Scripture, the deepest, truest knowledge we can get of her is from reading and pondering the tributes paid to her in the liturgical prayers the Church has composed for her. Note, for example, the Secret prayer in the Mass for the Assumption:

"Lord, may God's mother help thy people with her prayers. We know that she has shared the lot of humankind, and left this world; but let us feel that amid the glories of heaven she pleads our cause before thy throne, through the same Lord Jesus Christ."

In the third group, we have her patronal feasts: those commemorating her special interests or patronage. These are: the Queen of the Apostles, Saturday within the Octave of the Ascension; Queen of all Saints and Mediatress of all graces, two different Masses, both

---

[1] The translations quoted from the various Masses are taken from the Missal in Latin and English, edited by Rev. J. O'Connell and H.P.R. Finberg, published by Sheed and Ward, 1948. The scriptural translations are by Msgr. R.A. Knox.

to be read May 31; a recently established feast, also for May 31, is that of Queenship of Mary; Queen of the Holy Rosary, October 7; Refuge of Sinners, August 13; Help of Christians, May 24; Health of the Sick, the Saturday before the last Sunday in August; Our Lady of Perpetual Succour, June 27, and Our Lady of the Miraculous Medal, November 27. In many of these we can find in her our own special patron, or we can join with those more fortunate (the Apostles and Saints) in honoring her. Especially comforting to us should be the Introit for the Mass of Our Lady, Health of the Sick:

"I am the salvation of the people; let them call upon me, in whatsoever affliction, I will hear them."

But the Introit for her as Queen of the Apostles fills us with awe at her majesty:

"His own building amidst the inviolate hills, the Lord loves Sion's walls better than any other home in Israel. City of God, how high the claim that is made for thee! Come then, praise the Lord, all you that are the Lord's servants; you who stand in the house of the Lord, in the courts where our God dwells."

Fourthly, we are privileged to celebrate feasts of her special characteristics: Our Lady of Good Counsel, April 26; Mother of Noble Love, May 31; Mother of Grace, June 9; Humility of Our Lady, July 17; Our Lady, Mother of Consolation, Saturday after the feast of St. Augustine; Our Lady, Mother of the Divine Shepherd, September 3; the Motherhood of Our Lady, October 11; the Purity of Our Lady, October 16; Mother of Divine Providence, Saturday before the third Sunday in November. Were we to have no other clue to her character, these feasts ordained for her would describe her adequately.

So, the missal furnishes us with our Calendar of Engagements with Mary. It also furnishes us with an abundance of material for meditation on her life and her soul, her guidance in the Church, and her mission to souls, so that we verify her claim: "He who reads my lesson aright shall find in it life eternal."

A study of any one of the Masses composed for her will convince us that if we "read her lessons aright" we are on the right path in our search for eternal life. Let us take, for instance, one of the lesser known feasts, that for May 31 — Our Lady, Queen of all Saints and Mother of Noble Love:

The Introit, from Psalm 83, urges the daughters of Sion to go forth and behold their Queen "at whose beauty the sun and the moon are in wonder, and all the sons of God are glad." And because of her loveliness, it concludes: "Lord of hosts, how I love thy dwelling place."

The Collect asks that we may love God in all things and above all things on earth, and may in heaven enjoy glad fellowship with the saints.

The lesson or Epistle, is particularly poetic, for the Church, divinely guided by the Holy Spirit, has applied to Our Lady what the sacred writer says of wisdom. It gives us what we may call Mary's philosophy of life, her chart for the guidance of the Church, her credentials in her mission to souls:

"No vine ever yielded fruit so fragrant; the enjoyment of honor and riches is the fruit I bear. It is I that gave birth to noble loving, all reverence, all true knowledge, and the holy gift of hope. From me comes every grace of faithful observance; from me all promise of life and vigor. Hither turn your steps, all you that have learned to long for me; take your fill of the increase I yield. Never was honey so sweet as the influence I inspire, never honey-comb as the gift I bring; mine is a renown that endures age after age. Eat of this fruit and you will yet hunger for more; drink of this wine, and your thirst for it is still unquenched. He who listens to me will never be disappointed, and he who lives by me will do no wrong; he who reads my lesson aright will find in it life eternal."

The Gradual speaks of the crowning of Mary. The Alleluia implores her: "Come, our Queen, come, Lady, into thy garden; thy raiment is fragrant beyond all spices."

The Gospel is the affidavit of our claim on her, when the dying Christ gave her to John and through John she received as legacy the care of us. As a result of this bestowal, the Offertory contains our Lady's plea:

"Come to me, all you little ones; . . . come, eat my bread, drink the wine I have mixed for you."

The Secret implores that, sustained by her protection, we may be delivered from present ills and those to come.

The Communion prayer addresses her directly:

"Most rightful Queen of all the world, Mary ever virgin, intercede for our peace and safety, thou Mother of Christ."

In the Postcommunion we ask that God who gave us a safe-guard and protection in the most blessed Mother might also reward with the crown of everlasting glory us her children who observe her feasts.

Could we, then, ever doubt Mary's love and the power of her intercession? Is it not as though, through all the year, she is reversing the *Memorare* to assure us:

"Remember, O my children, that never was it known

that anyone who fled to my protection or implored my intercession was left unaided."

The Introit in honor of Mary, Mediatress of all graces, confirms this assurance:

"Let us come boldly, then, before the throne of grace, to meet with mercy, and with that grace which will help us in our needs . . . I lift up my eyes to the hills, to find deliverance."

3. EVERYDAY LITANY FOR MARY

Queen of our winning and our losing,
Queen of decision and of choosing,
    Teach us Wisdom's ways.
Queen of planning and waiting events,
Queen of ascending and dull descents,
    Bring us to trust-filled days!
Queen of hazards and of chances,
Queen of love and enduring romances,
    Make us wholly pure and free.
Queen of silence and fertile thought,
Queen of projects with zeal interwrought,
    Make us live our life in thee.

II

1. OCTOBER

The month of your Rosary, Mary — which makes it a beautiful month no matter what nature says about it, but just at present nature is flaunting her most beautiful autumn colors for you.

In the class room, the Sisters in the lower grades have taken down the beginning-to-get-dingy decorations which they put up to welcome the young ones back to school. Now they are putting up all sorts of devices and decorations about the Rosary, with injunctions to say it frequently and piously. The high-school bulletin boards are aflame with pictures of you — great Madonnas painted by your favored sons — and also pleas to be zealous about helping the missions both spiritually and financially. The college girls meet casually in the chapel; and when two or three or more have assembled, they say the Rosary in common. Since Father Peyton's campaign, sweet Mother, we have had an increase in the family Rosary, or in community-get-together rosary of any kind.

Way long ago we had family Rosary. I can't say we felt any very edifying devotion, but we'd kneel in my mother's room at night and say it — at her insistence. I remember my darling older sister Lillian who knelt close to the window (for air) and her very loud voice went singing out to the neighborhood — no harm in this, certainly, except that once in a while she had to yawn, but she didn't interrupt the prayers just for that, so there were some very peculiar sounds coming from her during the extent of the yawn. Then LeRoy and I — gigglers — would accidentally twist the phrases, be overcome with amusement, and be brought back to sobriety by our mother's stern rebuke. But we *were* faithful to the Rosary, Mary.

The beads are such a comfort in sickness. So many times our old Sisters twine them around their fingers. I doubt if some of them can get as far as one Hail Mary; but they make a prayer to you just by slipping the beads through their poor, stiffened fingers.

Then there's such a consolation in the Rosary while traveling. Way-back-when in the horse-and-buggy days, my aunt was driving with two friends quite a long distance over the (then) deserted country roads. A terrific storm came up, and her two companions were panicky. The horse, our famous gleaming black Nick, frightened at the flashes of lightning and the crashes of thunder, reared and plunged. She must have been a good driver, that aunt of mine, because she not only managed to control poor Nick, but with her Rosary twined in one of the hands holding firmly to the reins, she began to pray. Her two friends (non-Catholics) cried out — "Oh, teach us what to say! Teach us to pray!" That was as good a time as any to learn the Rosary and its efficacy.

My brother-in-law's chauffeur was a Polish Jew, converted to Catholicism by his determined wife. He was taking us once on a visitation, and on the way, my partner and I recited the Rosary. Mike joined in — he was so proud to join in, and "Holy Mary" boomed along to bless the traffic. He said: "Wait till I tell my wife that we said the Rosary along the way! But I'll have to say it with her again before we go to bed."

So many, many stories, Mary, have been told about
the power of the Rosary. The one I include here is
blessedly true, though I admit I fictionized it a little
bit:

2. BELATED KNIGHT FOR OUR LADY

He was young, he was a Capuchin, and he was on
the wrong side of the street that marked the boundary
line of the Monastery parish. The young woman who
opened the door when he rang the bell looked so
startled that he said:

"Am I in a Catholic household?" Then he noticed
the Rosary in her hand and smiled.

"Yes, Father, won't you come in?" She was quiet,
but tense, as though awaiting some event of great importance, and he talked rapidly to put her at her ease:

"I am Father Charles. I have come to take the census
and also to solicit support for our missions. When I
turned into this street, I realized that it must be the
northern boundary of our parish and that perhaps I
should not call on anyone on this side, but your house
is one of three in this block, and I thought it wouldn't
hurt to try."

He smiled a boyish, appealing smile, but before she
answered, the rasping voice of an old man was heard
calling from the upper floor:

"Margaret! Is that a priest you're talking to?"

"Yes, Father, it is," answered the young woman, and
before she had time to explain, the voice came again:

"Well, send him up. No, don't you come with him.
Send him up alone."

"Would you mind?", she asked. "Will you go up to
see my father-in-law? He's . . ." but her voice qua-

vered, and she turned away, leaving the visitor to find his way to the old man's room.

"You wanted to see me?", Father Charles asked pleasantly, and then stood quietly before the wasted figure in a faded bathrobe half sitting, half reclining in an easy chair. The old man looked at the sandled feet, the brown robe, the cowl, and then his eyes traveled to the pointed beard, the fair face with its deep-set blue eyes. When he finally addressed the visitor, he made a surprising remark:

"So Mary is really the Mother of God!", he exclaimed.

"Why — yes. Did you doubt it? She is the Mother of God — and our mother."

The invalid pointed with his stick toward a nearby chair, and when Father Charles, drawing it closer, had seated himself, the old, dark-veined hands were raised to cover a wrinkled face while the quavering voice went on:

"I am a sinner, a presumptuous sinner to ask a test of her, but how else was the faith to come? Father, will you baptize me? There is water in that pitcher over there."

"But, my dear fellow, not so fast! I cannot baptize you until I know more about you, and find out whether you have the requisite dispositions and knowledge. Tell me what this is all about."

"Father, all my life long I have been pursued — fiendishly pursued — by a doubt of Mary's sinlessness. Yet I could not ignore her as others seemed to do. Our family were members of the Episcopalian church. As a young man, I left the church because I felt the minister was getting too 'high church'; that is, he was beginning to introduce rituals and ceremonies that aped the Catholic Church. When he spoke of Mary as the Mother of God, that decided me, and I left on a quest for what I called 'pure doctrine,' unadulterated by superstition and idolatry. I tried all the sects that preached the so-called 'full gospel.' Later I married and raised a family, still without finding that which I sought. When my son became a Catholic under the influence of that young woman you saw downstairs, I was sure he was being fatally deluded. But further acquaintance with her made me respect and trust her. Through her, peace, order, and beauty reign in this home. However, while I occupy my time teaching my grandchildren their catechism; while in my research I studied all the history and claims of the Catholic Church, there was still one thing that kept me from falling on my knees and making my submission whole and entire. I could not believe that God could have a Mother — and not being able to curb my intellect to such a preposterous fact, I felt there was no use going further."

"And what has changed you now?" asked Father Charles.

"Father, I had a partial stroke last week; I don't want to disturb the members of my family who have been so kind and affectionate to me — chiefly through the influence of my daughter-in-law; but I know the end is near. I cried out almost in despair: 'Dear God, are You going to let me die like this — still fumbling, still groping in the darkness of unbelief?' The idea came to me to ask for a sign. Perhaps it was wrong, or perhaps it was just what God wanted me to do. I leave that to Him. Anyway, when Margaret came to make my bed about a half-hour ago, I said to her, 'Margaret, if by the power of that Rosary you are always saying you can get me a priest, I will make my submission to the Catholic Church and by God's grace I will die a Catholic.' She smiled at me, finished making the bed, and then said, 'All right, Father, I will go downstairs and say the Rosary for you.' That, as I said, was only a half hour ago, but it seems ages ago. But, Father, faith came before you actually came up to this room. When the doorbell rang, I said to myself; 'Why, I do believe. What a goose I am! Whether that is a priest or not, I do believe, Holy Mother, that you are the Mother of God and that you will obtain for me the grace to die a happy death.' Tell me, Father, how did you happen to come?"

The priest explained, and then he asked a few questions on the fundamental truths of salvation. Satisfied, and realizing indeed that the old man had not long to live, he went over to get the pitcher of water, and poured a little on the old man's head, saying the words as he did so:

"If you are not baptized, then I baptize you, in the name of the Father, and of the Son, and of the Holy Ghost, Amen."

Margaret was just rising from her knees when he descended the stairs. She smiled, but there were traces of tears on her eyelids: "It was the third sorrowful mystery that brought you, Father," she said, "and then I finished the rest of the decades in thanksgiving. Did you . . . ?"

"Yes, I baptized him," said Father, and then he added: "If I were you, I'd get the parish priest to bring him his First Holy Communion tomorrow. I will go back to the monastery and fill out the baptismal certificate. He — I suppose you know it — has not long to live."

"Yes, we knew it, but we didn't know whether he

knew it; and O Father, we have been praying so hard! Tomorrow is Sunday — I shall keep his Baptism a secret until I can get the pastor to bring him Holy Communion, and it will be a lovely, lovely surprise for everybody, because his favorite grandchild is making her First Communion, too. Thank you, Father, and will you accept our contribution for the Missions in thanksgiving?" She handed him an envelope and then knelt for his blessing.

As the caller left, he turned his face up to the clear blue sky in jubilation. He was young, he was fired anew with priestly zeal, and he knew that, for Our Lady, there is no wrong side of the street.

So much for that, Mother. I know the story might be criticized so far as right procedures are concerned, but it is the way it was told me first.

Then there is this article on various methods of meditating on the Mysteries. Because constant repetition is apt to grow into prayerless routine, I have figured out various ways of holding the attention. It may sound complicated, Mary, but I hope it is feasible — it has certainly helped me, and perhaps it will encourage your clients to devise even better ways:

3. WAYS OF MEDITATING ON THE MYSTERIES OF THE ROSARY

The variety of God's creation, and of His manifestations in that creation, is infinite. So, when He endowed His image man with memory, will, and understanding, He imprinted or emplanted within him a capacity for reproducing this variety — according to each individual's limitations, of course. That is why as we meditate day after privileged day, we can still find a fresh approach, fresh inspiration, fresh concepts — not that we can give God any new ideas for Himself! — but we can renew by variety our own enthusiasm, so as to be happy in the worship and love we offer Him.

Outside of the refreshingly startling ideas of God, only one person — could have thought up the Rosary — His Mother. And, in willing conjunction with a few of her privileged children, she has given it to us as it exists today: the beads, each decade separated by a larger bead, the little tail piece with its three small beads flanked on either side by a larger bead — and the Crucifix. That is the instrument itself. In the use of it, there are vocal prayers: Creed, Our Father, Hail Mary, and Gloria. In combination with these vocal prayers there are mysteries to be meditated upon: fifteen of them. These three items (the beads, the prayers, the mysteries) constitute *the Rosary* which the Church has richly indulgenced, and which forms the most popular devotion for all classes of Christians today.

Considered separately, not one of these items is exclusively characteristic of the Rosary. The Orientals, the Mohammedans, and pagans all had and have some sort of mechanical, material beads, pebbles, prayer wheels whereby to measure and count prayers. The four vocal prayers can be said (and are said) again and again apart from the Rosary itself. Meditation can of course be done without the aid of book, beads, or any exterior device. It's easy — when you know how and have the grace!

The Mysteries themselves are events in the life of Jesus and Mary. But in regard to *meditation* on these mysteries, a difficulty arises. Human beings are so constituted that they like monotony and routine in one sense — some fuss-budgets even hate a change in schedule or the re-location of a chair — everything should go on the way it's always been! On the other hand, a constantly repeated act or word tends to bring on ennui, distractions, and a search for change.

That is why there are offered here five suggestions for meditating on the Mysteries in order to fix the attention, avoid routine and distraction, stimulate the imagination to perform its part.

Four of the methods, briefly outlined, are:

I. To fix the mind on the composition of place for each mystery.

II. To consider the virtues to be imitated, vices to be avoided in connection with each mystery.

III. To recall phenomena of nature manifested in each mystery.

IV. To unite with the persons involved in each mystery.

V. The fifth method might be called interpolation, which is no new way of itself, but a suggestion for keeping the mind on one of the other four ways mentioned.

Needless to say, not all methods are to be put into effect at one time; neither should any of them be held to if it does not accomplish the three objectives mentioned.

I. Composition of place may be developed as follows:

The Annunciation: Mary's house at Nazareth, its setting, surroundings, neighborhood — a view of the garden:, "God loves a garden!" Evidences of springtime.

The Visitation: The hill country, Elizabeth's house, luxuriant growth of summer, Mary loves hills and mountains — in all her manifestations the locale has been hilly, rocky, or mountainous.

The Nativity: The hillside, the crowded town, the noisy inn, the stable. Winter, chilling winds, darkness, and then the contrast of mysterious light.

The Purification: White walls, steps, pillars, courtyard of the Temple flashing in sunlight, late winter with a hint of springtime. The Gate Beautiful.

The Finding of our Lord in the Temple: The Temple itself — its previous associations. Return from it, the roadway, the caravans — Seasons? There is no "feast" of the finding of Jesus — the season may be any that appeals to the imagination.

The Agony: Olive trees, the murmuring water of the brook Kedron, the cave, the rock, the garden, "God loves a garden!"

The Scourging: Pilate's house; the pillar in the court-yard.

The Crowning with Thorns: Soldiers' barracks; the plaza, the stairway to Pilate's house.

The Carrying of the Cross: Jerusalem; the road to Calvary, dusty, rocky paths.

The Crucifixion: Calvary, the bare hill, the tomb nearby.

The Resurrection: The tomb unsealed, the garden, "God loves a garden!" The road to Emmaus, the Cenacle, the crowded streets.

The Ascension: Roadway from Jerusalem, Mount Olivet, Heaven.

The Descent of the Holy Ghost: Jerusalem, the Cenacle, the crowded streets.

The Assumption of Blessed Mother: John's home, the scene of our Lady's death, whether in Jerusalem or Ephesus.

The Crowning of our Lady: Heaven.

II. Virtues or vices connected with each mystery:
Annunciation: The angel: obedience, exactness in delivering his message, humility before the creature who was to be his Queen. Mary: humility, faith, readiness of compliance. Both: an ardent love of God, a clear concept of the importance of His will, abnegation of self.

Visitation: Mary: charity, neighborliness, zeal, generosity, courage in facing the hardships of the journey. Elizabeth: hospitality, appreciation, faith, humility. Both: clear-sighted understanding of the Scriptures. Zachary? Poor Zachary!

The Nativity: Joseph: brave fulfillment of duty, humility in the face of rebuffs, thoughtfulness for Mary, trust in God; The Shepherds: piety, devotion, faith. The Magi: faith, preseverance, generosity. Mary: patience in enduring cold and discomfort, consideration for St. Joseph, for the shepherds, and for the Magi, forgetfulness of self, joy and gratitude in embracing her Son. The Bethlehemites, especially the innkeeper: coldness, hardness of heart, indifference, inhospitality.

The Purification: Joseph: humility and acceptance of poverty; Mary: self-effacement, exactness in fulfilling the law; Anna and Simeon: devotion, worship of God, fidelity to His precepts and inspirations.

Finding in the Temple: Mary and Joseph: self-accusation for possible neglect, joy and self-effacement at recovering the Child; Jesus: obedience to His father's will, zeal for the spread of truth; the Doctors: eagerness for knowledge of divine things.

The Agony in the Garden: Jesus: submission to the Father's will, perseverance in prayer, meek acceptance of the Apostles' indifference and drowsiness; the Apostles: indifference, sloth, yielding to physical comfort and heaviness of spirit in the face of temptation.

The Scourging: Jesus: fortitude, meekness, patience; Pilate: injustice, time-serving, culpable blindness; the soldiers: brutal cruelty; the Jews: jealousy, envy, revenge.

The Crowning of Thorns: Jesus: meekness, patience, endurance; the soldiers: cruelty, mockery, jeering.

The Carrying of the Cross: Jesus: patience, perseverance, consideration of others even in suffering; Veronica, Simon, the Holy Women, and Mary: sympathy, courage to do good in spite of opposition, thoughtfulness; the soldiers and the Jews: blind persistence in evil, brutality, cruelty.

The Crucifixion: Jesus: forgiveness of evil, thoughtfulness for others, submission to the Father's will; Longinus: faith and courage in confessing it; the Good Thief: courage, humility, faith; the Bad Thief, Jews, and Priests: pride, boasting of power, taunting cruelty, arrogance, and presumption.

The Resurrection: Jesus: worship of God, forgiveness of injury; the Apostles: dullness of heart at first, then submission, faith, and joy; the Jews and the soldiers: deceit, hardness of heart, denial of the known truth, lies, bribery.

The Ascension: Jesus: generosity in the promise of the Holy Spirit; understanding of the Apostles' sorrow at parting with him, patience with their continued expectation of an earthly kingdom; the Apostles: humble profession of faith, joy in the Lord.

Descent of the Holy Ghost: The Apostles: exuberant acceptance of His gifts, docility to His inspirations, conformity to grace, surrender to God's designs on their souls, zeal.

The Assumption of Mary into Heaven: Mary: ardent worship of God and desire to be re-united with Him;

Apostles: devotion to Mary, sorrow at parting with her, gladness for her release.

The Crowning of Mary in Heaven: Mary: joyful acceptance and performance of her mission as mediatrix of graces, Queen of the Apostles, of the Angels, of souls; Kings, patriarchs, prophets, and Angels: gratitude to the Holy Trinity for making Mary the daughter of the Father, Mother of the Son, Spouse of the Holy Spirit — and their Queen.

III. Phenomena of Nature Manifested in the Mysteries:

Annunciation: A simple maid understands angelic language and becomes perfectly attuned to the divine will. A virgin conceives.

Visitation: An unborn baby understands the language of heaven and leaps in his mother's womb; Mary breaks her native reserve and chants her "Magnificat."

Nativity: Humble shepherds hear and understand the language of heaven; truth-seeking wise men are guided by a star. "The earth trembles and is still."

Purification: Simeon and Anna learn to speak the angelic tongue of prophecy.

The Finding in the Temple: A mother's heart is broken, but learns the joy and mystery of the "Father's business"; a Boy of twelve astounds the learned men of the law.

The Agony: Drops of blood, like sweat; the rabble hurled to the ground at the sound of the Holy Name; the mystery of perversity!

The Scourging: Omnipotence withholds the flail of His anger, allowing man to exercise puny human power in flailing uncreated Power.

The Crowning with Thorns: Divine wisdom encircled

by stupid cruelty — and Nature herself does not protest.

The Carrying of the Cross: Human nature supported by Divinity only that it might endure more — for love.

The Crucifixion: Darkness at noon; the dead arise; "The earth trembles and is still." The Temple veil is riven.

The Resurrection: The stone of the tomb is, as it were, hurled from the opening of the tomb by the very emptiness within; "eyes were held" — notably those of the soldiers, of Mary Magdalen at first, and of the disciples going to Emmaus.

The Ascension: Gravitation has no power over a Body that has conquered death. "The earth trembles and is still."

The Descent of the Holy Ghost: The wind; the tongues of flame; Apostles' gift of tongues; thousands understand the heavenly message, no matter what their native language.

The Assumption: Jesus communicates to Mary His own agility and independence of the law of gravity, endowing her body with the attributes of eternity.

The Crowning of Mary: Pure spirits pay homage to the tangible body of the Maiden; all her senses are attune to the atmosphere of Heaven; "The earth trembles and is still."

IV. Dramatis Personae of the Mysteries.

The Annunciation: Gabriel, Mary, the Holy Spirit, the Heavenly Father, Jesus, the Incarnate Word; Isaias, who prophesied "A virgin shall conceive." St. Joseph, St. Ann, St. Joachim.

The Visitation: Mary, Elizabeth, Zachary, the unborn Precursor, Jesus, David, whose Psalms are re-echoed in the "Magnificat,"; Ruth, Judith, Esther, and Anna, mother of Samuel.

The Nativity: Gabriel, the multitude of the heavenly hosts, the shepherds, Wise Men, Joseph, Mary, Jesus, the innkeeper, Adam and Eve, whose long waiting was fulfilled.

The Presentation: Mary, Joseph, Jesus, Simeon, Anna, the High Priest, the Holy Spirit, the Prophets, and all the infants who were presented at that time; the Holy Innocents.

Finding in the Temple: Jesus, Joseph, Mary, the Doctors of the law.

The Agony in the Garden: Jesus, Peter, James, and John, Judas, the other Apostles, the young man who fled when the soldiers tried to capture him, Blessed Mother, who waited and wept, Malchus, whose ear was healed.

The Scourging: Jesus, Pilate, who scourged Jesus *because* He was innocent; the High Priests, Herod, the Apostles, St. Peter, who was weeping bitterly; Blessed Mother, who waited and watched and wept; the soldiers.

The Crowning with Thorns: Same as above; Judas, who saw that He was condemned and tried to retract.

The Carrying of the Cross: Jesus, setting out on the road to Calvary; Pilate's wife, who warned her husband; Judas, who went and hanged himself; Veronica whose veil formed "a banner and a bandage for the world"; the holy women whom He comforted; Simon, who helped him carry the cross; John, hurrying to repair his desertion; Blessed Mother, who never deserted.

The Crucifixion: Jesus, Mary Magdalen, Mary of Cleophas, Blessed Mother, Dismas the good thief, the thief on the left hand, John, Longinus, the soldiers and priests, the souls released from Limbo.

The Resurrection: Jesus, Mary, Mary Magdalen, the Holy Women, Peter and John, Thomas, the other

Apostles, the disciples on the way to Emmaus, the group of Apostles on the sea shore, the five thousand to whom He appeared in Galilee.

The Ascension: Jesus, Joseph, Ann, Joachim, and John the Baptist, Zachary and Elizabeth, who welcomed Him in Heaven; The Apostles, Mary.

The Descent of the Holy Ghost: Jesus who sent Him; the Holy Spirit, Blessed Mother and the Apostles, the thousands converted by Peter's sermons.

The Assumption: Mary, the Angels, especially Gabriel; Jesus, the Holy Spirit and the Father, Ruth, Judith, Esther, Eve.

The Crowning of Mary: The Holy Trinity, Mary, the angels, patriarchs, prophets, Holy Innocents, Confessors, Virgins, and martyrs whose Queen she became.

V. Interpolation.

This, as has been said, is no new method of meditating, but is a suggestion for keeping the mind on one of the other four. It is for private devotion and is by no means an offering of a "Hail Mary" different in form from that approved by the Church. The method is carried out by inserting some little phrase pertaining to the mystery at the appropriate parts in the Hail Mary. A few examples are given:

Hail Mary, *to whom Gabriel came at Nazareth,* full of grace, the Lord is with thee, etc.

Or: Hail Mary, full of grace *and full of sorrow at the scourging of Jesus,* the Lord is with thee, etc.

Or: Hail Mary, full of grace, the Lord is with thee *particularly in His Resurrection,* etc.

Or: Hail Mary, full of grace, the Lord is with thee, blessed art thou among women *especially in your Assumption into Heaven,* and blessed is the fruit of thy womb, Jesus, etc.

Or: Hail Mary, full of grace, the Lord is with thee, blessed art thou among women, and blessed is the fruit of thy womb, Jesus, *who was crowned with thorns,* Holy Mary, etc.

Or: Hail Mary, full of grace, the Lord is with thee, blessed art thou among women, and blessed is the fruit of thy womb, Jesus, Holy Mary, *crowned Queen of Heaven,* Mother of God, etc.

Or: Hail Mary, full of grace, the Lord is with thee, blessed art thou among women, and blessed is the fruit of thy womb, Jesus. Holy Mary, Mother of God *and spouse of the Holy Spirit,* pray for us sinners, etc.

The interpolations are made at different places for the purpose of holding the attention and preventing the very device itself from becoming routine.

Queen of the Holy Rosary, pray for us!

Well! So much for your Rosary, Mary. There are still volumes to be said, but to go on with the rest of your feasts this month: The feast of your motherhood comes on the eleventh. That's a feast added comparatively recently, but like so many others, one wonders why it wasn't proclaimed long ago. This feast was instituted to celebrate the fifteen-hundredth anniversary at Ephesus: the proclamation that you are really and truly the Mother of God. As Pius XI said in announcing the establishment of the feast:

"All of us who are united to Christ and members of His body were born of Mary with our head. She is the Mother of us all, spiritually, but truly Mother of the members of Christ."

He that made you rested in your tabernacle, Mary, and He said to you: "Let thy dwelling be in Jacob, and take root in my elect."

October twentieth there comes a feast under your

lovely title "Mater Admirabilis." It has a proper Mass for the Religious of the Sacred Heart, but we can rejoice in it, too, Mother, and in the lovely fresco in one of the cloisters of the convent of the *Trinità dei Monti* in Rome. Here you are depicted as seated in a court of the temple, the symbol of purity — a lily — at your right, and a distaff, a work-basket, and a book of Sacred Scriptures at your left. Oh Mary, Mother of good housekeepers, it is surely comforting that you are represented so many times not only at prayer, but also at the homely duties so common to women the world over! Yet the Epistle for the Mass of this feast would seem to point to pure contemplation:

"Arise, my love, my beautiful one and come. My dove in the clefts of the rock, in the hollow places of the wall, show me thy face, let thy voice sound in my ear; for thy voice is sweet and thy face comely."

There's no conflict here; it's just another of the many, many suggestions that true contemplation overflows into active zeal. You are His dove, His love, His beautiful one, but you gave your fingers to weaving, and to any other homely occupation that claimed your attention.

4. A CROWN FOR THE QUEEN

Annunciation:
>The angel came to greet the maid
>With words that made her shrink, afraid:
>>*How can this be? I know not man,*
>>But Gabriel showed her God's great plan,
>And Mary bowed in full accord:
>*Behold the handmaid of the Lord.*

Visitation:
> Over the hills in haste she swept,
> Her joy hidden, her secret kept:
>> But Elizabeth at their embrace,
>> Echoed the angel's *full of grace*
> And Mary's words to Heaven soared:
> *My soul doth magnify the Lord.*

Nativity:
> The shepherds watch upon the hills,
> When lo, the air with brightness fills:
>> The angels sing of peace on earth
>> In the Saviour's lowly birth.
> To Mary sent, by all adored,
> *This day is born to you the Lord.*

Presentation:
> The temple of Jerusalem
> Unfolds its doors to welcome them.
>> Simeon chants his parting song
>> After his waiting, trusting long.
> His words in Mary's heart are stored
> And still she magnifies her Lord.

Finding in the Temple:
> *Why didst thou leave us thus, my Son?*
> The grief of three days' loss was done
>> In joy at finding Him again
>> Amid the scribes and learned men.
> And His return was their reward:
> Subject and Son was Christ their Lord.

Agony in the Garden:
  Father, if Thou wilt, remove the chalice!
  Withhold this draught, distilled by malice —
        But He arose, encouraged, strong,
        To face the ravening, traitorous throng:
  Heed not My will, Thine own be done,
  Thy victim I, *Behold Thy Son.*

Scourging at the Pillar:
  I find no cause in Him was said,
  And yet they lashed until He bled.
        I'll scourge Him then, and let Him go!
        (Coward Pilate's puppet show!)
  The wanton farce was then begun:
  My God, behold Thy sinless Son!

Crowning with Thorns:
  The makeshift twist of branch and thorn,
  The heavy weight all meekly borne,
        His royal head, unbowed as yet,
        Its share of torment now must get.
  No part of suffering does He shun,
  Behold the Man, O God, *behold Thy Son!*

Carrying of the Cross:
  Bearing His own cross, forth He went
  His head still crowned, His garments rent.
        Blood and spittle stain His face,
        And yet for men He still begs grace.
  The ghastly gauntlet must be run:
  Father, aid Thy willing Son!

Crucifixion:
> *They know not what they do!*
> Still for pardon does He sue:
>> *This day in Paradise . . . I thirst*
>> As though from love His heart must burst —
> Father, receive at last Thy Son,
> The price is paid, the Victory won.

Resurrection:
> Early the first day of the week,
> The women came, His tomb to seek.
>> But the stone rolled back aroused their fears,
>> And only the empty tomb appears.
> *Fear not! Rejoice, for He has risen!*
> Freed at last from sin-barred prison.

Ascension:
> He lifted up His hands and blessed them,
> His words of hope and love caressed them.
>> But a cloud received Him from their sight,
>> And angels, clad in garments white,
> Recalled to them the prophets' story:
> He would return in regal glory.

Descent of the Holy Ghost:
> The days of Pentecost were passed
> In prayer and praises, alms and fast,
>> When suddenly a mighty sound
>> Filled the house and streets around:
> The Holy Ghost, in tongues of fire,
> Came down to comfort and inspire.

Assumption:

I will speak my works to the King.
My Mother, tell this wondrous thing:
　　In you the works of God are praised,
　　Your body and your soul He raised
To dwell on high beside His throne,
Yet still we claim you as our own.

Crowning of Mary:

A crown of glory for your head,
The Father's love upon you shed,
　　Your Son to usher you to bliss:
　　O Mother, grant your children this:
In heaven at last to see your face,
O stainless maiden, Queen of grace.

III

1. NOVEMBER

This month, Mary, starts with a joyous honoring of
all the saints who have not a special feast or a special
Mass of their own — or for that matter, an honoring of
all the saints who *have* special feasts and *Masses* and can
be venerated yet again as a sort of echo to their glory.
You, my Mother, are the Queen of Saints, but in a special sense. An earthly queen is of the same "breed" as
the lowest of her subjects. Elizabeth II of England,
dear as she is to her subjects, and her queenship acknowledged by all the world, is still queen only by ac-
cident of birth and circumstances. Not you, holy Mary.
We are told that if all the merits of all the saints: virgins,
martyrs, confessors, doctors, widows (why aren't wid-
owers made special mention of?) — if all these merits
were added together, yours would still surpass the ag-
gregate. These astronomical calculations, while I bow
my intellect to them, leave me cold. I just like to think
of you and salute you as the Queen of all saints, and to
pray to you that one day, through your prayers and
merits, I may come to the company of all those saints
— and of you, our Queen.

Francis Thompson has a lovely thought (but ex-
pressed in a very awkward quatrain) that when the
astronomer drops his tube and opens his eyes to the
heaven above the stars, he discovers the brightest star of
all — you, O Star of the Sea. The same could be said of
any specialist: the doctors of the law will be welcomed

by you, who fulfilled every "jot and tittle" of that law.
The physicians will hail you "health of the sick!" The
writers will greet you "Our Lady of Literature." Sweet
Mother, our comfort here below, there is not one field
of endeavor in this our exile that will not find its fulfillment in you, "our tainted nature's solitary boast."

By a transition sudden and so characteristic of much
of the Liturgy (reflecting as it does both the ways of
God and our own human vicissitudes), the next day: all
the flowers and decorations are removed, the altar is
plain and stark in its majesty. Commemoration of all
souls — a plea to remember them, and to meditate on
our last end. Father told us in Retreat that death is a
paradox in this: it is certain, but the time is uncertain;
it is an end and a beginning, a punishment, yet a reward; a curse, but also a blessing.

I should like to think of it, Mary, as only a comforting certainty: the time is unimportant if I spend my
days in union with His Divine Will. It is a beginning
— a first faint beginning with you and your blessed
Son. It is a reward — not because I've done anything
which really merits a reward, except in you and because
of your promise. "Those who explain me shall have
everlasting life" is applied to you, though it was
originally spoken of wisdom, and I have tried to explain you both to myself and to others. Again, there
is your scapular promise: those who wear the scapular,
you said to St. Simon Stock, will be released from
Purgatory the Saturday after their death; and I have
tried to fulfill the conditions holy mother Church lays
down for the attaining of this glorious assurance.
Death a blessing? What a blessing it will be! Not
that I want to die merely to get rid of a few pains
and annoyances and frustrations in this life. These

I take gladly since the joys and satisfactions are so, so much greater in comparison.

So, sweet Mother, I'll see you the Saturday after my death. Meanwhile, I pray that you will intercede with your Son for the holy souls that are awaiting their release: relatives, friends, those who are there perhaps through my own fault, those who have none to pray for them, those who are nearest (or farthest) from their release. The list is so long!

Toward the end of November comes our American holiday of Thanksgiving. I'm told its institution was an attempt by the Puritans to do away with Christmas with its (as they considered it) idolatry and pagan customs. *They* should see the commercialism of both feasts today! But with the adaptability so characteristic of our nation, we have incorporated Thanksgiving within our customs, and have kept Christmas too. The Church in her age-old adaptability has accepted this American-made feast and has made it possible for her children to draw spiritual profit from it. Only, of course, every day is really Thanksgiving Day for the children of the Church. And how much *I* have to be thankful for: for restored health, for mind and soul attune to beauty, for vocation and all its attendant graces, for restoration to grace when I have strayed from the pathway of your Son's commandments, and for temporal things: friends within and without the community, congenial occupations, and all the luxuries, spiritual and mental and physical that comprise the hundred-fold your Son promised me.

Your thanksgiving, Mary, was embodied in your Magnificat which you were to chant when you were only fourteen or fifteen years old — perhaps after about twelve years spent in the Temple. But your Song of

songs was a summing up of all that had gone before,
a recognition of the joyous present, a confidence for
the days to come. "Take three tenses," Mary — foreshadowing the culmination in that completely satisfying NOW of eternity.

This month, on the twenty-first, comes the feast of
your Presentation in the Temple.

Tradition says you were three years old. There is
a picture of you painted on the side wall of the sanctuary in St. Ann's Church, where as a child I used to
go. I loved to look at that painting: Joachim and
Ann at the foot of a long flight of steps, Joachim looking stolid and somewhat resigned; but Ann's arms and
Ann's straining mother-glance are stretched to you, as
though to hold contact as long as possible. She made
that charming little girdled-in dress for you, Mary,
just as Anna of old made for her Samuel a little coat
that would protect him from the chills and damps of
this same Temple of God. At the top of the steps,
framed in a colonnaded doorway, a venerable old man,
presumably the High Priest, stands waiting to greet
you. And you — oh, three-year-old Mary — you are
depicted half way up, your flowing hair covering most
of that fine-textured white dress at the back, your
hands crossed upon your breast (perhaps even then
you were saying within your heart: "My soul doth
magnify the Lord"), and your little-girl face tilted upward in eagerness.

How the dwellers in the Temple must have loved
you! I compare you with the three-year-old children
of today. You were sheltered from the many accidents
that happen so tragically often to children now: a
little girl recently dashed out from her own home in
play — a truck ran over her, crushing her horribly

within the very sight of her "safe" home and her screaming mother. Even though the traffic in your day, Mary, was comparably great, what with camels and chariots, and dashing horses and not pedestrian paths, even though (as we are told) in your times there was a harsh disregard of human life, I cannot believe there were so many hazards for a child of three.

For instance, there are the diseases of today — diseases which our crowded way of life makes all the worse. Yes, they tell us infant mortality was greater in your day. At least today we have decreased the danger of childbirth infection — but there still seem many more opportunities to contract infections!

I like to think, Mary, that your little body was well-nourished, well cared for, and physically fitted for the part you were to play in our lives as co-redemptorist. And how lovely is the body of a three-year-old well-formed child!

Not so long ago, I was in the parlor visiting with a relative who brought her two-month-old baby to see me. I was holding the infant, loving his innocence, his helplessness, his carefully-made clothing, when a little child of three whose mother was visiting another Sister came running over to me. The baby attracted her. She made gurgling noises to it, and with complete unconsciousness of self (or of me, for that matter!) she stood on my feet in order to get a better view. I carefully removed my newly polished Sunday shoes from her feet, but she, all unconcerned, groped for them again so as to raise her chubby little body. All she wanted was to contemplate the infant nestling so contentedly on my lap.

You must have loved babies, too, Mary. You must

have seen them in the Temple when their parents brought them to ransom them: boy babies forty days old, girl babies twice that old, bought back from the Temple by the price of two turtle doves if the family was poor, or by lambs if the parents could afford it. Perhaps you lingered around, hoping for a chance to take the babies in your arms, just as Simeon and Anna did years later with your own dear Son.

They probably extended you a warm welcome within the Temple precincts, Mary. After the High Priest had greeted you with dignified formality (but surely he smiled a little at you, lest you be frightened) he turned you over to the care of the women.

I like to think their welcome might have been somewhat like that extended to me at my entrance into religion, when I skipped up the hill with my suitcase so anxious, so anxious to have these doors close upon me safely; while my mother, my darling mother — anxious and solicitous about many things — called me to wait for her. She was forty-four years old at the time, Mary — probably your own age when Jesus left you to begin His public life.

The cordiality of my welcome was so unexpected. I was surprised that total strangers would pop at me, kiss me on both cheeks, and tell me they had waited for me so long. I, in my crass ignorance, began to think I must be important indeed, to get all this attention! All I had hoped to do was to slip in unnoticed among them, get clothed in a postulant's dress, find my way around, and slide into the routine somehow or other. Of course, common sense should have assured me that my every step and every minute would be watched and guarded and directed by Novice Mistress and fellow novices and postulants. So it surely was with you, Mary — there must have been some sort of regulations and routine into which you were inducted lovingly and understandingly by older companions.

It wasn't however, mere unpersonalized routine. That welcome you received, Mary, was tempered according to your own individuality. You were pure and without sin — so perhaps were many of the children in the Temple; that is, they were naturally innocent! You were charming and polite and docile; so were many others in your group. Undoubtedly you were intellectually keen: later, twenty-four years and all the Joyful Mysteries later — it is recorded of you and St. Joseph, "they understood not the word He spoke to them", but these were things you pondered in your heart, Mary, and the frank avowal of not understanding is a trait of intellectual honesty.

The point here, though, is that while your characteristics conformed in general to those of the others, yet it wasn't as a type or a symbol, or as a prissy little "goody-goody" that you joined others in the Temple service. You found your place there and you dwelt with those around you according to the Mary-ness of Mary, so that when your teachers, companions, or guardians found some special act of generosity, or thoughtfulness, or cleverness from you, they could say: "How like Mary! Only Mary could have done that!"

Apart from your divinely endowed traits, sweet Mary, I claim that you were a very human person: witty, capable of sparkling conversation (certainly your Son had ready answers!), retiring perhaps, but not with the shyness of self-consciousness; good-humored, tactful, but all in your own Mary-way; surely a good companion at recreation, but always with the God-consciousness that completely penetrated you:

"Thus have I gazed toward the sanctuary to see Thy power and Thy glory." (Psalm 62)

Was there a change in the way of dress for you, Mary, in the service of the Temple? Was there a uniform or some sort of clothing by which is was made known that you were thus dedicated?

My own street dress was examined so curiously by my Novice Mistress after I had exchanged it for the postulant's dress and cap and was preparing to put the secular clothing in that suit-case my mother was to take back. My Novice Mistress liked especially my hat — a little blue velvet thing with a long white feather. She herself had been a milliner, and I think the tastefulness of it appealed to her. See, she was human like you, Mary, and the little details of a homely life she did not scorn. She knew, too, that getting rid of that hat was no sacrifice for me — I was only too anxious to exchange it for the postulant's cap, with its net veil flowing behind me to my waist.

These exterior details were very unimportant, though, compared to the things of the spirit. My Mistress taught me to meditate, Mary — the first meditation she prepared with me was on the Presentation of our Lord in the Temple. She dwelt upon the fortuitousness of Simeon's entrance, of Anna's appearing, just at the very moment that the Holy Family appeared.

And you, my Mother Mary, you were only three at your entrance, but I think you were more matured than children of my times, and so perhaps they taught you to read; or orally they began to teach you the long and glorious history of your race. That is why my sketch, "Meditation of Mary," can't be too, too much a matter of fantasy?

2. MEDITATION OF MARY

Mary's activity in the performance of her Temple duties never hindered her from her favorite occupation: that of gathering words into her heart and "pondering" over them. *Conferans* is the Latin word used in the Gospel — she conferred within herself about divine truths and their possible application.

When she selected fruit from the orchard for the supper of the Priests and the Temple officers, she looked at the pomegranates, the figs, and apples, and some parallel thought from the Scriptures was sure to echo in her mind:

"Let my Beloved come into his garden and eat of the fruit of his apple trees." (Canticles 5:1); or perhaps: "Let us see if the vineyards flourish, if the flowers be ready to bring forth fruits, if the pomegranates flourish." (Canticles 7:12)

Again, exulting in the holy silence and peace that gave her opportunity to recall the Priests' teaching, she repeated the wisdom of Solomon:

"To speak a word in due time is like apples of gold on beds of silver." (Proverbs 25:11)

"Mother of all the living," she whispered in recalling Eve (Genesis 3:20), but she shuddered at the result of Eve's curiosity and her treacherous persuasion in causing Adam to break God's command. Then there was the threat of God to the serpent:

"I will put enmity between thee and the woman and thy seed and her seed; she shall crush thy head, and thou shalt lie in wait for her heel," (Genesis 3:15), and Mary looked down at her own heel, pink against the rough sandal, and trembled to think of its contact with cold evil. As she remembered God's word to

Eve: "I will multiply thy sorrow and thy conceptions; in sorrow thou shalt bring forth children." (Genesis 3:16), she sympathized with the woman, even while recognizing the justice of the punishment.

(Ah, Mary, thine own sorrows were multiplied to expiate for sins and stains not thine!)

"Mother of all the living," she whispered, "I would gladly be thy handmaiden."

Lover of beauty as she was, she recognized that extraordinary beauty was a sign of special predilection among the women of the Inspired Writings. She dwelt in delight upon the account of Sara and the great charm that even in her old age aroused the admiration and desire of Abimelech; so much so that Abraham feared the king of Gerara would kill him in order to possess her. (Genesis 20:1)

Then came Rebecca in this garland of praise, this shining wreath of glory to God for the models He had caused the Holy Spirit to place before her — Rebecca who came down to the well and in sweet courtesy offered drink to Abraham's messenger, welcoming him with the gracious words:

"Drink, and I will give thy camels to drink also." When Mary served water and wine to the Priests at their supper, she thought of this, and she murmured the Holy Spirit's praise of Rebecca:

"An exceedingly comely maid, and a most beautiful virgin." (Genesis 24: 4-16)

She loved the account of Rebecca's hospitality when in answer to the messenger's question:

"Tell me, is there any place in thy father's house to lodge?" she replied eagerly:

"We have good store of both straw and hay, and a large place to lodge in."

(Mary, Mary! Later you will hear the harshly un-gracious reply: "We have no room in the inn.")

Mary's artistic sense was gratified in the picture of Rachel and the sheep. She thought of this when she helped the Levites prepare the sheep for the sacrifice, and she recalled the story:

"And behold, Rachel came with her father's sheep; for she fed the flock . . . Rachel was well favored and of a beautiful countenance . . . and though Jacob served seven years for Rachel, they seemed but a few days, because of the greatness of his love." (Genesis 29:9 ff)

Mary meditated over that long, long love story of Jacob and Rachel — a love so enduring that at her death the very springtime was turned into sadness when Jacob buried her in the highway that leads to Bethlehem; and he recalled its poignancy many years later in giving orders to his sons to bury him there in the cave with her. (Genesis 35:19)

(Mary of the beautiful countenance, you will pass by her tomb on the way to that stable outside Beth-lehem, and it will not be springtime, but cold and barren winter; but the Child in your womb will turn the sadness into exuberant joy.)

Mary, grinding wheat for the showbread in the Temple, remembered the story of Ruth — Ruth who returned with Naomi her mother-in-law to the land of Israel; Ruth who gleaned in the fields and became the wife of Booz: "That she may be an example of virtue in Ephrata, and may have a famous name in Beth-lehem." (Ruth 4:11)

(But Mary! Her name is famous only because she is one of your ancestors; it is your name that is the most

famous in all Bethlehem, and Bethlehem is famous
only because of you and your Son's birth there.)

When she sat in the Temple workroom among the
maidens, sewing the fine linen used for the priestly
garments, it was the story of Anna that Mary pondered
upon; Anna, Elcana's wife, whose womb the Lord had
made barren and whose rival therefore afflicted her;
Anna, who prayed before the Lord in such grief and
urgency that Heli the High Priest thought her intoxi-
cated. But when she made known to him the cause of
her sorrow, the Priest turned prophet and assured her
that the God of Israel would grant her petition. And
indeed, within the next year, she conceived and bore
the son she called Samuel. But in her joy she did not
forget the Lord's generosity; hence she told Heli:

"I have lent him to the Lord all the days of his
life."

Many times Mary repeated the words of Anna's
thanksgiving song:

"My heart has rejoiced in the Lord . . . they that
were full before have hired themselves out for bread,
and the hungry are filled . . . the Lord kills and makes
alive . . . the Lord makes poor and rich, humbles and
exalts. He raises up the needy from the dust and lifts
the poor from the dunghill . . . the Lord shall judge the
ends of the earth, and he shall give empire to his king,
and shall exalt the horn of his Christ."

(Mary, Mother of the word, it was this song that
formed the basis of your Magnificat — but how your
inspired gratitude transmuted it into exquisite poetry!)

It was this Samuel who became the strong judge of
all Israel — yet what a lonely little boy he must have
been, as "a child, ministering in the sight of the Lord

before the face of Heli, being girded with a linen ephod." Anna, having "lent him to the Lord" still did not relinquish the sweet privilege of ministering to his physical needs, but made him a "little coat, which she brought to him on the appointed day when she went up with her husband to offer solemn sacrifice." (I Kings 1:28-2/19)

It was this coat that Mary mused upon — she compared it to the mystical coat of diverse colors which Jacob had made for his favorite son, Joseph. She thought if she had a little son she too would dedicate him to the service of God, and she would use her fine skill in weaving to make for him a seamless robe.

The sacrifice of Jephthe's daughter caused sadness to Mary. This little girl, immolated to her father's rash vow, was not even given an authentic name, and yet in Mary's time, nearly twelve hundred years later, the Temple maidens still played a game in her honor, with timbrels and dances such as the little girl had used to welcome her father back from his victory over the Ammonites. Mary thought to herself that she would not have asked "two months, that she might go into the mountains to bewail her virginity" (Judges 11:37) before the sacrifice should be consummated — she would offer her life gladly in thanksgiving for the victory of Israel, and in plea for its continued safety. But ah! that daughter of Jephthe was so sweet and joyous, so graceful and vivacious!

(Mary, Mother of Sorrows, thou hast not spared thy life by reason of the distress and tribulation of thy people, but hast prevented our ruin in the presence of our God.) (Judith 13:25)

When Mary heard the Priests and Levites speaking of the iniquity of Herod, and of his interference with the religious privileges of the Jews, she longed to be another Esther, to appear before the King in all the charm of her youth, to win his heart and incline his favor for the protection of her race.

But when she learned of the Romans' conquest, and their atrocities against the sacred Temple, then did she pray that another Judith would arise to use her own wealth and beauty and fortitude in overcoming the enemy, and to inspire the Priests with confidence in God's power to save his people. How humbly she would salute such a valiant woman with the praise once given to Judith: "Thou art the honor of our people . . . for thou hast done bravely, and thy heart has been strengthened, because thou hast loved chastity . . . and therefore also the hand of the Lord strengthened thee, and therefore thou shall be blessed forever." (Judith XV pass.)

(Mary! Blessed art thou among women, and all generations shall and do indeed call thee blessed!)

And when Mary lifted up her pure heart to her eternal Father, asking His will for herself, He leaned down in delight to answer her:

"Be the mother of all the living; be beautiful as Sara, Rebecca, Rachel, and Esther. Be as self-sacrificing as Jephthe's daughter, faithful as Ruth, valiant as Judith."

And Mary answered with her favorite ejaculation — an ejaculation so frequently in her heart and on her lips that years later, at the decisive moment of her life, the reply came forth spontaneously:

"Behold the handmaid of the Lord; be it done to me according to Thy word." (Luke 1:38)

IV
1. DECEMBER

This month, my Mother Mary, might be said to contain the epitome of your life. First, of course, there is the feast of your Immaculate Conception. What volumes have been written on that! Shortly after Pope Pius XII proclaimed the Doctrine of your Assumption, someone dug up this story:

A very high-up and influential person is quoted as saying: "Of all times! The most incongruous and inappropriate! This marks the end of the Catholic Church." The writer of the story goes on to say, in substance:

When was this dire prophecy made? Not recently. It was back in December, 1854, when Pius *IX* pronounced and defined that you, sweet Mother, "in the very first instant of your conception, by singular privilege and grace granted by God in view of the merits of Jesus Christ, were preserved free and untainted from original sin."

People are always predicting the end of the Catholic Church. Why don't they look back and find out how many unfulfilled predictions have preceded theirs?

In all the exuberance of His creative energy, Mary, I think God enjoyed the creation of you. That is why we keep harping back to the quotations from Proverbs: "The Lord possessed me in the beginning of His ways." That is why this little handmaid of yours, a faint shadow of the creativeness of God, enjoyed writing the fantasy that follows: "Little Lower than the Angels."

2. LITTLE LOWER THAN THE ANGELS

Whistling a joyous tune, God set about creating the material universe. The Whimsical Angel regarding Him with raised eyebrows:

"Lord dear, what are You going to do with all that trash?"

"H'mm?" answered God. "What am I . . . oh — I'm going to use it to manifest My glory so that the visible things of creation might show forth My perfections."

"But to whom?" persisted the angel. "We already know those perfections, and we show forth Your glory. Who . . . ?"

"Well, yes, that's so — there'll have to be a rational creature among these hills and waters and trees. Let Me see — I might even get you angels to serve him . . ."

At this, Lucifer, who had been contemplating his own perfections shrieked out in desperate pride:

"Not on Your life! *I* will not serve . . ."

Thereupon Michael found that suddenly his indignation became a flaming sword, and he darted at the rebellious one with lightning swiftness. As Lucifer continued to hurl his defiance, Michael shouted:

"None of that now! Stop it this very point of eternity!"

The conflict of Lucifer's rebellion and Michael's attack created a fiery blast that singed the quivering angels' sensibilities and the stench thereof offended their nostrils. In an endeavor to save his place, Lucifer clutched at those who were willing to support him; and hence a third of the heavenly host in their tragically mistaken loyalty fell with him into the mounting flames.

Their departure clarified the atmosphere, and in the peace and stimulating calm that followed, the remaining angels broke forth into hymns of praise and thanks.

"You will not serve?" reflected God. "You poor fool, you'll spend your eternity in serving. Now — where was I before that interruption? Oh yes — there will have to be a creation, part animal so that he can rule over this visible kingdom, part spirit so that he can hold intercourse with Me and My angels."

He spun in His hand a lovely, lashing wind, and turning to the Whimsical Angel, He said:

"Here — catch!" The angel found himself involved in a disturbing, playful element that disrupted his equilibrium quite a bit until he got the hang of it. Then, seizing the part most easy to grasp, he flew all over creation, whipping up the clouds, lashing the waters, hurtling great rocks in the sudden power of its onslaught.

"O God, what fun!" he laughed, "let me have charge of the winds, will You?" There ought to be wheat fields that I can blow them across, and blue waters that I can tip with white caps; and look — see what lovely shapes I can make of the clouds. Will you give me charge of them, too?"

A smaller angel asked: "Then let me have charge of the skies, God, will You? And the sun and the moon and stars? I'll put them out for You on time, and guide them in all their appointed places. I'll make the morning stars sing together for You, and when You call them, I'll see to it that they answer cheerfully: *Here we are, to do Your bidding.*"

"Why, you darling little angel, are you sure you can manage them? We-ell, see what you can do at first. Trail them across the sky, manage the traffic for them, get the Whimsical Angel to intervene with clouds according to season and to taste. Perhaps the Color

Angel will help you with the dawns and sunsets.   I
think you will like the monotony of it."

"And me?" queried a wistful angel. "God, will You
let me be the Color Angel?   I'll splash the trees with
crimson and gold, dye the grass to suit the eye of the
beholders, and lavish various shades on the flowers."

"Oh here, you angels go on with yourselves!   Why
don't some of you take charge of the animals?   Timid
Angel, that can be your job.   I'm going to have lions
and tigers and things like that.   And trees?   Let Me
see — Stately Angel, you can take charge of the trees.
You will love the redwoods and beeches and oaks.
Vary them according to season, and be sure to have
some that will stay green all winter.   The Color Angel
will help you.   Then — h'mm — let Me see," God puck-
ered His brow and thought a mighty thought:

"I shall make man according to My own image.   I
shall impress My spirit upon him; but since he's to
rule the universe (if you angels ever get it started),
I'll have to give him a body — and he'll have to rule
that, too."

The angels, remembering Lucifer, ventured a question:

"But, great God, are You going to give him free
will?   That's a fearful weapon to put into his hands."

"My Goodness!   What good would he be to Me without free will?   I want someone who can interpret the
voice of creation in terms of praise; and of what use
is praise unless it is offered freely and intelligently?
However, I shall give him a test at first, to make sure he
understands his freedom."

So God scooped up a handful of clay that the Wind
Angel had dried sufficiently for it to be malleable, and
the angels hovered in admiration while He sculptured

arms, legs, a torso, and a head with flowing hair. They uttered a cry of gladness when Adam, having received the breath of life, fell on his knees in rapt adoration before his Creator.

But Adam was lonely. With all Paradise before him, with the angels to amuse him, he himself could not explain the restlessness and longing that possessed him.

God knew what was wanting. He put His arm about Adam and soothed him into sleep. Then from his side, painlessly, He drew a rib from which He formed a most beautiful body. And when Adam reacted from the anaesthetic, lo! there was a lovely woman sitting beside him, waiting for him to rouse and play with her.

"There you are," said God, dusting His hands. "Now — run around this garden I've given you; make up names for all these animals and birds and flowers and plants. Only thing is — don't eat of the fruit from that big tree you see in the center."

God withdrew for a while, to give them a chance to get acquainted each with the other, and to see how the angels were getting along with the charges He had given them. But suddenly all heaven glowed with an angry light, and the angels, ceasing their joyous activities, covered their faces. God roared through the re-echoing depths of creation:

"What the . . .? That devil of a Lucifer has tempted My creatures to disobey My law. Now there'll be the devil to pay, indeed! You — you two with your petty excuses — get out of My Paradise. Where is that flaming sword Michael used against Satan? But no — wait a bit . . ."

God did not want to drive them out naked and unprotected as they were. He gathered some fig leaves

from the tree the Stately Angel offered Him. While
He was threading His needle, the Timid Angel came
to Him with the complaint that his charges were getting out of control. They were roaring something terrible!

"H'mm?" said God. "Well, you'll have to keep them
away from Adam and Eve for a while; I can't have
humanity fed to the beasts just yet. Drive 'em into the
forest and let 'em eat grass."

Then God gave His children garments of fig leaves.
Adam's He made to hang from one shoulder and reach
just to his knees, while Eve's He made in a circle
around the neck, gathered to the waist, and flowing
to her feet. Eve plucked a trailing grape vine to adorn
it as she hurried from Paradise, but it singed and
withered as it floated behind her against the flaming
sword with which Michael pursued them until they
reached the outer confines of Eden. He barred the
entrance against them.

God looked after them with a worried frown.

"Now I shall have to redeem them," He said, "but
not yet. Man had his choice, and he sought the fruit of
knowledge of good and evil. I shall let him find in
long ages of repentance just how bitter that fruit can
be. Then in the fullness of time I will give him knowledge of Me and My mercy. I shall take a human form
and become like to him, so that I may raise him at
last and make him like unto Me. Now, in order to do
that, I shall have to be born of a human mother . . ."

The angels swept around Him exultingly: "Oh, let
us help You make Your Mother," they caroled. "Look,
we'll make her taller than the skies, more majestic than
the redwoods, powerful as the wind . . ."

"And I," said the Angel of the Interior, "will cover

her with the finest jewels and most sparkling gems now forming in the depths of the earth."

God laughed.

"You ridiculous angels," He said, "I want a woman, a mother such as I planned Eve to be, *in whose bosom's depth of comfort a man might base his head.* What was it the Wind Angel said about wind sweeping over the wheat? We'll make her hair something like that — wind-swept wheat in the sunshine. And you, Color Angel, save your choicest bloom of rose for her cheeks, and the sky's deepest blue for her eyes. Don't think, however, that she's going to be a perpetual statue on a pedestal, or a pretty picture on a holy card. She's going to be at first a real, little baby, born of real parents, and then a little girl; and then — just as she is growing into womanhood, I shall send one of you to ask her if she'll let Me be born of her. Ah! She must be beautiful, to mirror forth the beauty that shall be within. Pink and blue — I shall give her France for her dowry — I think France would like that."

"Don't you mean England, Lord?" ventured a Nordic Angel.

"Well, both of them. The whole world can be her footstool, for that matter. She can plant her footsteps here and there, and wherever the imprint of her heel is made, Satan shall be crushed, and grace for mankind will spring forth. There, Satan, you've over-reached yourself, as will always be the case. You promised men they should be as gods — I shall raise them to the Godhead through the grace of Mary, My Mother."

The Recording Angel plucked a quill from out his wing to write the records of God's promise. The Angel of the Emerald Isle stood before the throne, and he danced a little jig.

"And sure, Lord," he wheedled, "couldn't You make her to be born of the Irish race?"

"Now by My sacred power! The Irish will dominate the face of the earth, angel dear, and if I made My Mother of their nationality, there'd be no holding them down at all, at all!"

Gabriel wheeled great flashing flights of joy through the empyrean and began to rehearse the velvet words of his greetings:

"Hail, full of grace!"

There, my Mother, is my syncopated version of God's activities in regard to you.

Let learned doctors go deeply into the Scriptural evidence, the tradition, the exact sense in which the word "conception" is used, the fittingness of the doctrine, and all that. We, thy lesser children, rejoice in the words of the simple hymn:

> "O Mother, I could weep for mirth,
>   Joy fills my heart so fast,
> My soul today is heaven on earth,
>   Ah, could the transport last!
> I think of thee and what thou art,
>   Thy majesty, thy state,
> And I keep singing in my heart:
>   Immaculate, Immaculate!"

The Mexican artist, José de Ibarra, Mother, has a lovely picture of you called "The Conception of the Virgin" — only, as — in so many cases, your Immaculate Conception seems to be confused with your miraculous conception of the Man-God; but perhaps his plan is to foreshadow your motherhood. The picture is worthy of contemplation in its suggestion of graceful activity.

You, Holy Mother, winged, are represented as coming down from the Eternal Father with the Child already in your arms. The Child is looking and stretching upward as though loath to leave His heavenly home; but you are gazing down upon the globe around which is entwined the serpent. At your right crouches St. Michael equipped with sword and shield — and *he* is making very sure that the venomous evil does not crush *your* heel.

That was a puzzling expression you said to St. Bernadette, Mary, when she was commanded to ask your identity. "I *am* the Immaculate Conception." The savants of that day turned the words over and over in their minds and on their tongues: "I *am* the Immaculate Conception" — not "I am one who has been immaculately conceived," or "I am, as the Church teaches, free from original sin." While you said those actual words, Mary, in the peasant language that Bernadette could understand, yet for her to have made them up out of her imagination would have been wildly impossible.

By the way, Mary dear, that reminds me of something I've been pondering over: the recorded words we have of you during your Scriptural lifetime are all so different from the words you spoke to privileged souls afterwards. Outside of your Magnificat — which was certainly flamboyant and self-confident enough! — all your Scriptural words are so humbly self-effacing: "Behold the handmaid . . . thy father and I have sought thee sorrowing . . . they have no wine."

For that matter, the Scriptural words that your Son is recorded as saying to you seem to belie all the power and grace and majesty He has given you. I say this in absolute acceptance, of course, of the interpretation the Church wants us to put on these words; but, taking them face value, they certainly need interpretation! A friend of mine says your Son spoke to you the way her children speak to her: "How is it you sought Me? — did you not know . . . Woman, what is that to you and to Me . . . My hour has not yet come."

Certainly, Mary, there seems no foreshadowing in the words themselves of all the power and majesty and glory He was to give you. For afterwards, in all your appearances, you say things like: "Build me a church here . . . let processions come . . . go tell the Bishop that I command . . ." O Mother of sublime self-confidence, taught by God-confidence, how wonderfully you work out your mission as Mediatress of Grace!

Your next December feast, sweet Mother, is that of the Holy House of Loreto — the 10th. That little affair is the sort of thing that causes us to exclaim: "Isn't that just like Mary." As Zsolt Aradi says, somewhat hesitantly, by way of introduction:

"The history of Loreto presents to believers and honest disbelievers one of those eloquent questions of faith ever posed to rational skepticism." That's a prudent way to approach the simple recording of facts: The House of Nazareth where Gabriel came to you, where you lived after your return to Egypt up to the time of your Son's beginning His public life, was uprooted by angels, taken to the Dalmatian coast, and later by the *same* angels (how could they know that?) transported to Loreto where it stands today inclosed in a huge basilica.

Some of the earlier authorities on your shrines and feasts do not mention this at all, sweet Mother, and those who do mention it insist that the history of Loreto is based partly upon tradition and partly on historically recorded facts. However, I prefer to be-

lieve that for some reason known only to the Divine
Counsel you and God wanted your house to be at
Loreto instead of at Nazareth; and it is only one more
instance of the importance attached to everything concerning you. The burden of proving the contrary is
on the disbelievers. The real mystery is why anyone,
in the face of all the circumstances connected with it,
would take the trouble to try to prove the story false.

Then the next feast is that of your Expectation —
the 18th. We do have December as the epitome of
your life, Mary, but we skip all around in the matter
of your age: first you are only a microscopic fetus in
the womb of Ann; then, in regard to your House you
are already some twelve hundred years old in the devotion of your children; and now we come to your
maturity: about the age of fourteen or fifteen.

Your Expectation, sweet Mother, is not celebrated in
the Missal for general use, but it is certainly a reason-
able sort of feast, and would find an echo of appreciation and comfort in the hearts of expectant mothers
the world over. It is commemorated so beautifully in
Father Fabor's hymn:

> Like the dawning of the morning
>   On the mountain's golden heights,
> Like the breaking of the moonbeams
>   On the gloom of cloudy nights,
> Like the secret told by angels
>   Getting known upon the earth:
> Is the mother's expectation
>   Of Messias' speedy birth.
>
>   ❖   ❖   ❖
>
> Thou hast waited, child of David,
>   And thy waiting now is o'er . . ."

Romantic, perhaps, in its metaphors, but oh, so sincere, and so clearly showing forth Father Faber's love of you!

On that day, the week before Christmas, you were journeying — traveling southward with St. Joseph, and he too knew that your time was near. He comforted you with the assurance that he would go slowly so as not to jolt your precious Burden; but he would waste no time in unnecessary delays, so as to get quickly to the Inn or to relatives who would take care of you.

You could reassure him, Mary. Perhaps it was your prayer that produced "no room in the inn," so that your Divine Son could be born in the privacy of that stable instead of in the raucous bustle of a public hostel. Much has been said about the heartlessness of that "no room in the inn" affair, Mary, but one consideration is: just as later He drove the buyers and sellers from the Temple, so in the beginning He arranged that you, His temple, should be free from the disrespect, the ruthlessness, the noise and bustle, materialism and commercialism that characterized the Inn. And just as, later, in the holy peace ensuing from His cleansing of the Temple, the little children broke forth in praises, so in the silence of that holy hillside the angels burst forth into song and praise — song and praise heard only by shepherds childlike and simple of heart. They were childlike and simple of heart, Mary, but also they had you, the Seat of Wisdom, to procure for them the understanding needed; that is why I wrote for you the discussion: "The Shepherds Understood," trying in my limited way to ferret out just what it was that they understood.

3. THE SHEPHERDS UNDERSTOOD

"They understood of the word that had been spoken
to them concerning this child." Here is the summing
up of divine paradox. From the angel's message, the
glory in the sky, the heavenly harmony, they might
humanly expect a palace, lights, music, grandeur, and
magnificence. But no — they found a baby with his
mother; and *they understood!*

Now, some spiritual writers have taken an extreme
view of the poverty and discomfort of that manger:
earthen floor, rough walls hewn from the cave, chilling winds, darkness, and the filth and odor characteristic of any ordinary stable. Others have taken a
more optimistic view, and have written that the stable
was not much more uncomfortable than the inn itself;
that St. Joseph with his carpenter's skill, Mary with her
domestic art, must certainly have arranged it so that it
was neat, clean, and habitable. It had the additional
advantage of offering more privacy than the inn with
its promiscuous confusion.

Whichever theory is tenable, we still have this mystery to ponder: *Why* the sight of a poor couple, a new-
born child laid in the feedbox should bring about an
understanding of the angel's message.

First of all, was there something they had *mis*understood?

Shepherds as a class are not stupid men. True, they
have to deal with the most stupid of animals; but, as
all teachers know, the lower the intelligence quotient of
the pupil, the greater is the intelligence required to
teach it. To put it logically, a moron might con-
ceivably teach a genius something, but it would take a
genius to teach a moron anything. Shepherds, further-

more, have the limpid simplicity, the penetration, and acumen peculiar to men who are much alone in the long watches of the night. They acquire a basic wisdom from their very dealing with fundamental issues, untrammeled by admixture with such extraneous ingredients as luxury, ambition, and frivolity. Besides, these shepherds – Jewish, and backed by a long and honorable tradition – must have considered it quite natural that the first announcement of a Messiah should come to them, since he was to be of the race of the shepherd king: David.

But – David, after all his pastoral and military experiences, *was* a king, surrounded by luxury and comfort. He even reproached himself with it, as he said to Nathan:

"Dost thou see that I dwell in a house of cedar, and the ark of God is lodged within skins?"

Yet the abundance of wealth which he had heaped up, he bequeathed to his son Solomon, so that the Sacred Writers delighted in enumerating the many horses, camels, flocks, the vast amount of silver and gold, the elegant and exquisite workmanship and skill at his command.

Hence, there was this element in the angel's story that was puzzling to the shepherds on Bethlehem's hills:

"You shall find the infant wrapped in swaddling clothes and laid in a manger." They were even given this information as a *sign*.

The brilliance faded, the music of Heaven's choirs trailed off into silence. There remained only the distant stars, the chilling winds, the sheep undisturbed and unaware of divine revelation. So the shepherds' natural reaction was:

"Let us go over to Bethlehem; and let us see this word that is come to pass, which the Lord hath showed to us."

No hesitation there — no time lost in confusion and doubt. They were men of action:

"They came with haste."

Then shone light — light more brilliant than that which blinded them at the beginning of the revelation; only this time they did not fear. Then sounded melody — music more compellingly beautiful than that produced by the heavenly army; only this time it was clear and attuned to their increased grace. For the light and the music were within their own souls:

"And seeing they understood of the word that had been spoken to them concerning this child."

Perhaps an echo of the Shepherd-King's self-reproach helped their understanding: "Dost thou see that I dwell in a house of cedar, and the ark of God is lodged within skins?"

The ark of God — nay, God Himself — was lodged within the skin of humanity, and God's power in limpid simplicity was manifested to these wise men of humble penetration.

By the same token, we too can come with haste — come with the urgency of our many needs, and find that God is lodged among us: in gold or silver, in cedar or in less precious material, He dwells among us — our food and our sufficiency — to administer to our necessities. And when we come with haste, with the light and music of faith and grace in our souls, we too will understand:

"For by the mystery of the Word made flesh the light of thy glory hath shone anew upon the eyes of our mind; so that while we acknowledge him as God

seen by man, we may be drawn by him to the love of
things unseen." (Preface for the Christmas Mass)

Yes — Mary, they understood when they found Jesus
with you. But what a seemingly harsh return was
made to the shepherds' devotion! No sooner had you
become established in the village, known and loved
and at peace, when there came the message to Joseph:
"Arise, take the child and His Mother and fly into
Egypt."

Geographically, Mary, it seems very easy to trace
your movements during this month of December:
your Conception, probably at Jerusalem, or Sephoris,
or Bethlehem itself; the flight of your House from
Nazareth to Tersatto (and appropriately enough it
was shepherds — Dalmatian shepherds, who found it
there,) thence to Loreto. And now: your easily trace-
able journey from Nazareth, through Jerusalem, to
Bethlehem, thence up to Jerusalem for your Purification, back again to Bethlehem to receive the adoration of the Magi; and then, because of their adoration
— hastily southward and eastward to Egypt.

Geographically, yes, Mary, it is easy to trace your
way. But it is very hard for a human heart to trace
the ways of God in the incident of the massacre of the
Holy Innocents. And you — journeying southward in
safety: did you know that the children of those shepherds who had befriended you were being dashed
against the walls, pinioned on the blunt swords of in-
human soldiers? Did the cry of those mothers (*Rachel,
bewailing her children, and would not be comforted,
because they were not*) follow you and echo in your
ears? December, Mary, that begins with the joyous
feast of your Conception, and continues through the
bittersweet of Christmas, ends with exile for you, and

grief for your friends and neighbors in Bethlehem.

In humbly confiding this problem to the mysterious ways of Divine Providence, we can find, spiritually, many explanations of it. One is in the Introit for the Mass of the Holy Innocents: "Out of the mouth of infants and of sucklings, O God, thou hast perfected praise, because of thy enemies." Perhaps these babies, had they continued to live, might have been among those who raised clenched fists in air, crying "Crucify Him! Crucify Him!" But the Gradual in this same Mass says: "Our soul hath been delivered as a sparrow out of the snare of the fowlers. The snare hath been broken and we have been delivered."

Some have felt that this fearful massacre was God's way of punishing the inhabitants for not receiving His Son. If that were so, perhaps the children of the shepherds were not among those killed. Either they had none under two years of age, or they had a way of concealing them among the hill caves.

December twenty-eighth was my own dear mother's birthday, sweet Mary, and each year from my entrance into the convent until her death, I made for her a spiritual bouquet, setting the number of Masses, Holy Communions, Acts, etc., according to the years of her age. Your own age, my Mother, during these December events was probably fifteen. Fifteen-year-old girls of today are in high school. They are beginning to "date" seriously — seriously in their own minds, if not in the opinion of their parents. They are making plans and dreaming dreams for their future. Present events loom large, though, and out of all proportion to their actual importance: the choice of class colors and a class motto; the removal of a favorite Sister-teacher;

or the *non*-removal of someone they consider partial or
strict or unreasonable in some way.

But oh, my Mother Mary, it is a privilege to handle
the youth of today. They are good — most of them, at
least most of those in our Catholic schools; and those
who are wayward are anxious and seeking and amenable to a friendly interest shown them. Usually those
we meet are pious, open, and frank, easily influenced by
constructive suggestions. What a privilege, and what
a heavy responsibility is ours in guiding them and
guarding them!

Our Lady of youth, pray for the youth of today.
You — you had your Present, Past, and Future curled
beneath your heart or lying cuddled in your arms
during all that eventful December. We have to take
those tenses separately, Mary; and for youth, the future
seems so long acoming! But for old age, the days go
swiftly, and the past stretches long, long back. For
all of us, the real grace is to tie the past and future in
the sacred present, fulfilling His will in the expectation of the all-embracing NOW of eternity.

Now, that twisting back and intertwining of three
tenses Mary, in connection with the prayer for youth
brings us back to a feast-day which I skipped: that of
St. John on the twenty-seventh. He was a favored
youth, if ever there was one! You did not have to
appear to him, my Lady, you were already with him
— for so many years! You did not have to say to him:
"Build me a church." This loved and favored disciple
was busy building a monument of words for your Son,
the Word made flesh, while you were keeping house
for him, keeping distractions away, refreshing his
memory and his spirit. Little did his own mother, the
wife of Zebedee, know about the true state of affairs

when she asked Jesus that John might sit at His right
or left hand when He came into His kingdom! The
wildest of ambitions could not have conjured up the
privilege that was his, when, exercising his gorgeous
talent — native and inspired — in writing his Apocalypse, his Epistles, and his Gospel, you, his mother-by-
legacy, were making for him a little citadel of privacy
and silence where he might pursue his work.

St. John, beloved disciple of the Word, pray to the
Mother of the Word for us.

Now, Mother of the Word, because so much of this
month is concerned with journeys, I shall end it with
the story of the Magi's Journeys.

4. MARY AND THE MAGI

There were three of them: Gaspar with his dream of
a queen so gracious and beautiful and wise as to
arouse all his ardor of chivalry and gallant service;
Melchior with memories of a childhood beautified and
ecstatically blessed by a wise and loving mother;
Balthasar sorrowing over the loss of a graceful and
winsome daughter whose charming ways had once
gladdened his life.

Now, there were four acts in the drama of the Magi:

   I.   They followed a significant star,
  II.   They followed it to find a King,
 III.   They found Him and gave Him gifts,
 IV.   They returned to their own country by a differ-
ent route.

Of these four acts, two of them concern a journey:
Up from Abraham's city of Ur; northward by a
scarcely perceptible road to Baghdad; across the Syrian

desert between the Euphrates and the Syrian border; stopping a brief while at Palmyra; thence onward to the city of Damascus; southward again, keeping east of the Sea of Galilee and of the Jordan until they crossed the ford near Jericho. This was the route of the three silent men, men who prayed and watched the sky as they journeyed onward in perfect accord.

And though they knew it not, Mary was the way.

Gaspar brought his treasure chest full of gold — a generous portion of the wealth that his noble family had passed on through generations; gold that had bought for them all the service, the delights, the abundance of food, clothing, lands, and the culture that had made for the members of his family an earthly paradise of peace and security. Gaspar came of a kingly family, royal in all but the responsibility of governing, hence free from the weight of power that sometimes saddens and darkens the life of an actual king.

But Mary was House of Gold, Queen of the King of kings.

Melchior's treasure chest contained frankincense — the precious gum resin that flowed from the trees growing seemingly without soil from the polished marble rocks in his native land of Carmania. His ancestral wealth consisted chiefly of these trees. He himself, skilled in the cultivation of them, had prepared his gift before setting out on the long journey. He selected the youngest trees, made a deep incision along the slender trunks, watched while the large, clear globules, amber and oblong (the shape of tears) oozed from the wounded bark; and then he collected it in his cedar-lined chest. Merchants all the way from Baghdad to Damascus valued this substance: it burned with a bright, clear flame, giving out a sweet odor. The Jews, he knew, made it a fourth part in the mixture of sacred incense which God Himself had taught Moses how to compound. But the Persians considered that it had medicinal properties: they used it to heal carbuncles and sores; before it attained a solidified state, they applied it as a plaster to heal leprous sores.

Oh, Mary, health of the sick!

It was Balthasar who brought myrrh in his treasure chest of delicately carved ivory. This myrrh was a bitter gum resin from his native Arabia, valued as an unguent and a perfume. Like the frankincense, it was also used sometimes as incense in sacrificial rite, but chiefly it was used in embalming. *And the name of Mary means myrrh.*

We may assume that these three were representatives of the three races sprung from Noah's sons: Shem, Ham, and Japhet. We may ponder over the significance of their gifts. The conventional practice is to consider that they represented the three aspects of the Saviour: His Kingship, His Priesthood, His humanity. It might be, too, that each Wise Man offered what was most precious to himself as a perfect sacrifice.

Whatever their race, whatever their origin, it is probable that these three were in the service of the Persian King as counsellors and scientists, learned enough in the ways of heavenly bodies to recognize instantly that the star which announced the birth of Christ was no ordinary star, no phenomenon explained by the conjunction of Jupiter with Saturn, or by the shooting across the heavens of an extraordinary comet. Well versed as they undoubtedly were in Jewish literature, they must have had in mind the prophecy of Balaam:

"A star shall rise out of Jacob, and a sceptre shall spring up from Israel."

So it must have been divine inspiration which enlightened them and inspired them to undertake a journey — the most fantastically chivalrous, the most blindly faith-testing of all pilgrimages in history. *Mary was the Way!*

The star was indeed significant, in that it told them of the coming of a King and guided them to Jerusalem. But they lost it there, and had to depend on human help — help which after all was deceitful, since the information was given them in hypocrisy and self-interest. Of the end of their search, of the performance of their errand, we are told only:

"Entering in they found the Child with Mary His mother, and falling down they adored Him; and opening their treasures, they offered Him gifts: gold, frankincense, and myrrh."

Presumably there was room for *them* at the inn — room for these stately, serious travelers with all their retinue, which must have been considerable enough to cause quite a traffic block in Jerusalem, since we are told that Herod was troubled "and all Jerusalem with him."

Perhaps it was in uneasy sleep at the inn, after they had presented their homage that, "being warned in sleep, they returned to their own country by another route."

That other route was most likely a way to the Jordan slightly southward so as to avoid Jerusalem and Jericho, or a roundabout way south through Beersheba, then east to the great highway (the Mecca Route) in the land of Moab and beyond the Dead Sea.

It has been estimated that the way from Persia to

Jerusalem was between one thousand and twelve hundred miles. The return journey, in their avoidance of more traveled routes, must have added at least three hundred miles to this. That is a great deal of traveling merely for the purpose of offering gifts and returning!

And what had they found? They had found the Child with His mother Mary. Mary was their way, their mediatrix. To her they gave their treasures; and Mary gave the gold to St. Joseph; the frankincense was stored away for offering to the Temple on their next visit to Jerusalem (they not knowing what a long, long journey they would take before seeing again the sacred Temple), and the myrrh in its ivory chest she took from the hands of Balthasar, gave him a loving, understanding glance, and placed it in the crib of her Son.

From her they received a return of gifts. They gave material things — she gave riches beyond even their knowledge and dreams of opulence. It was the thought of her that guided and sustained them on the way back. And whenever afterwards, on their return to their native land, they looked across the many miles to the west, they saw the stars shimmering across the sea, making a long pathway of silver light which broadened out toward them; and they remembered the Divine Child — with Mary His Mother.

For so it was that Balthasar brought myrrh in bitter remembrance, but was healed of his sorrow by Mary the Maid. Melchior brought frankincense in worshipful homage to the most beautiful of mothers; and Gaspar, offering his gold, found at last the perfect Queen to receive his most chivalrous service.

For Mary was then, as now, the Way to the Truth and the Light.

V

1. JANUARY

My sweet Mary, this New Year begins with the first shedding of your Son's blood. The ceremony of circumcision is depicted with spiritual significance in the Old Testament as the absolute cutting off from the worship of God all that might be considered idolatry or self-seeking. It is the binding tie between God and His chosen people, a symbolic purification of the body in the service of God. Actually (as is the case in so many of the exterior practices laid down by Moses), it was then and is considered today an advisable therapeutic procedure. But in those days, without benefit of sterile instruments, in fact with only a "sharp stone," it must have been a cruel operation.

"A bloody spouse thou art to me," Sephora exclaimed — though it was she herself who had seized the sharp stone when she realized that both her spouse, Moses, and his young son were in danger of death from the angel — an avenging death because of Moses' neglect to circumcise his son earlier.

But, as always when there is sacred sorrow, joy accompanies: for this day, Jesus received His Holy Name. It was St. Joseph who bestowed that Name, in accordance with the custom that the giving of the name was the father's prerogative: *"Thou* shalt call His name Jesus," the angel had said to Joseph. So completely accepted was this custom, that when Elizabeth said her son's name was to be John, the busybody neighbors appealed to the speechless Zachary, who had to satisfy them with the written confirmation: "John is his name."

So important is the giving of your Son's name, Mary, that the Church is not satisfied with celebrating it merely as an addendum to the Feast of the Circumcision. She has a special feast for it, either January second, or the Sunday occurring between January first and sixth. There was power in the proclamation: "John is his name" — power to loosen the tongue of Zachary and cause him to break forth in his exultant canticle.

But WHAT power there is in the name of Jesus! St. Paul exhorts: "In the name of Jesus, let every knee bow, of those that are in heaven, on earth, and under the earth; and let every tongue confess that the Lord Jesus Christ is in the glory of the Father." (Philippians 2:10-11)

Those on earth, yes. There was a time when your Son chose to demonstrate very specifically the power of His name. It was in the garden, after His agony, in answer to His question: "Whom seek ye?" And those very enemies who were seeking His life had to fall prostrate when they cried out: "Jesus of Nazareth."

On their return from their mission, the Apostles reported: "Even the devils were subject to us in Thy name!"

Aside from that spectacular power, it is so comforting, Mary, merely to bow the head and whisper: "Jesus!" But because of both the power and the comfort, what a shame, what a disgrace it is that it should be used blasphemously!

How horrible that those two blessed syllables should become merely an expletive, a mistaken show of strength, boldness, anger, or surprise. Your Son's name, Mary, is used indiscriminately with other ejaculations:

hell, or *God,* or some meaningless expression like *jiminy, gee,* or *gosh!* in the careless speech of today. Sweet Mother, obtain blessing and power for the Holy Name Society, so that its members may zealously correct this abuse. Obtain for all your children that they may live in the grace, the power, and the beauty of this holy name.

The next important feast for you in January, Mary, is the Epiphany — the manifestation of God to the Gentiles — the visit of the Wise Men from the East. What I have written in regard to them, and to you, and to their journeys, Mary, is fanciful — but it just might have been that way.

But now I am going to digress from these kings of Tharsia and the islands offering presents from the kings of Arabia and of Saba bringing gifts, to talk a little about your own journeys, Mary. Your January journeys are not so easily chronicled, for it is puzzling to reconcile the accounts in the synoptic Gospels. St. Luke's tells of Gabriel's visit to you in Nazareth, specifically a city of Galilee. At his hint about Elizabeth's condition, you take the eight-mile journey south to the hill country of Judea. Presumably you return after St. John's birth; then comes the decree of Caesar Augustus, your traveling to Bethlehem with Joseph, the trip to Jerusalem for the Purification; but then, St. Luke says after you had performed all things according to the law of the Lord, *you returned into Galilee,* to your city Nazareth. Not a word about the Magi, about Herod's trickery, the slaughter of the Innocents. On the other hand, St. Matthew, disregarding all those early days in Nazareth, speaks as though you must have been living in Bethlehem at least *two years,* else why would Herod have set that age limit in his command for the massacre of the Infants? Then St. Matthew tells about the refugee flight into Egypt; and according to him, it took a special warning to make St. Joseph settle in Nazareth instead of Bethlehem on his return from exile. Actually one would have thought his choice would naturally be Nazareth without any special revelation.

Father Joseph Husslein, in his *The Golden Years* has this explanation:

When St. Joseph discovered your pregnancy, he was not willing to "expose you publicly," and for that reason he undertook the journey to Bethlehem very much sooner than December in order to protect you from questioning looks or remarks of your neighbors in Nazareth. In other words, that decree might have come early in the spring, or the summer, and you and St. Joseph might have been living with friends or neighbors in Bethlehem, or in perhaps some lowly hut of your own. But when your time drew near, St. Joseph wanted to get better accommodations for you in the caravansary inn. Then, still trying to conceal the too-soon birth of Christ, he decided to remain in Bethlehem, but went down to Nazareth to make arrangements for closing up his business affairs there, perhaps selling your little property.

This supposition, Mary, ingenuous as it is, can be shot full of holes. According to many authorities, no inn of that day had any better accommodations for child-birth than the poorest home could have afforded. Many scholars tell us that the Jewish espousals were considered the equivalent of marriage, and therefore the birth of Christ was in order, so far as the neighbors reckoned the time. Certainly, if there were any irregularity here, our Lord's enemies would have spotted it and brought it up during His public life. No — it was left for the scoffers of today to bring up the question of illegitimacy.

So far as the other discrepancy is concerned, another scholar has this explanation: Since obviously Christ was the Son of David and was to inherit the throne of His father according to the angel's revelation, then St. Joseph might have considered that Bethlehem should be the place of their home. St. Luke, having omitted any mention of the Magi and the flight into Egypt, was simply putting forth the fact that Christ did live in Nazareth probably up until the beginning of His public life. St. Matthew, writing for the Jews, was more concerned with showing how the prophecies had been fulfilled:

"Thou, Bethlehem, the land of Juda, art not the least among the princes of Juda, for out of thee shall some the captain that shall rule my people Israel." (Micah 5:2) Secondly: "Out of Egypt have I called my son," (Hosea, 11:1) and thirdly: "He shall be called a Nazarene." This last is certainly an obscure prophecy, for actually in history it refers to the promise made to Manua's wife and the birth of their son Samson: "Behold, thou shalt conceive, and bear a son; beware thou drink no wine nor strong drink nor eat any unclean thing; for the child shall be a Nazarite of God from his infancy." (Judges 13:7)

Again, we are told that the Gospels are not meant to be a biography of our Lord in the strict sense; facts and circumstances were recorded only insofar as they exemplified the truths, the "good news" of Christianity which the Apostles were to announce. However, I leave these things for scholars to prove or disprove and like the Psalmist (with much more reason!) I may claim: "I busy not myself with great things, nor with things too sublime for me. Nay rather I stilled and quieted my soul like a weaned child. Like a weaned child on its mother's lap, so is my soul within me." Like a weaned child, Mary, not seeking earthly sustenance since my heavenly Father knows I have need of these things and will provide them, but seeking the peace and security of sheltering my soul within your care and protection.

Sunday within the Octave of the Epiphany, my Lady Mary, we celebrate the Feast of the Holy Family. Bernardino Luini has a beautiful picture of you in the midst of four other figures — suggesting thereby that you and Joseph and Jesus were by no means isolated. He makes your face so beautiful, Mary, beneath the transparent veil that comes just to your eyebrows, that for long the eye can dwell on nothing else. You are smiling. The lines of your cheek bones direct the sight down to that beautiful, generous mouth. Your chin is rounded softly, the tilt of your head is showing utter grace and sweetness.

But then the eye of the beholder is drawn to see what you are looking at: a very lively Infant on your lap is leaning over to a baby John, raising two fingers to bless with the right hand, while extending a playful left hand beneath St. John's chin. St. Elizabeth (depicted not quite so aged as one might expect) is looking at you, Mary, and her finger upraised seems to call attention to the upraised fingers of the Baby Jesus. To the right is St. Joseph, full of patriarchal dignity with his very large nose and bald head. One interesting detail is the strong family resemblance between you and St. Elizabeth, between Jesus and John.

It seems a very leisurely group, Mary, and there are no evidences of housekeeping around, as there are in

so many of the masterpieces of you. But the Feast of
the Holy Family does bring me to thoughts of you as
house-keeper. I cannot wholly credit the so-called
private revelations of some devout souls who have en-
visioned angels doing your housework for you — a
somewhat sublimate version of Snow-white and the
Seven Dwarfs, with those squirrels using their tails for
dusters! I'm sure the angels' wings would be good
feather dusters if they cared to use them that way (and
if they *had* wings) but I like to think you were the
valiant woman described in the Proverbs: Solomon
begins by asking: "Who shall find a valiant woman?"
somewhat as though he were in doubt that there could
be such a woman. Yet his description certainly seems
to fit not only the type or symbol he is seeking, but also
and very definitely you, Mary, in your own characteristic traits:

Far and from the uttermost coasts is the price of you.
The heart of your husband trusts in you and he shall
have no need of spoils. You will render him good and
not evil all the days of your life. You have sought wool
and flax and have wrought by the counsel of your
hands. With the fruit of your hands you have planted
a vineyard. You have risen in the night and given a
prey to your household and victuals to your maidens.
You have girded your loins with strength and have
strengthened your arm. You have seen to it that your
lamp shall not be put out in the night. You have put
out your hand to strong things, your fingers have taken
hold of the spindle. You shall not fear for your house
in the cold of snow, for all your domestics are clothed
in double garments. You have made for yourself clothing of tapestry; fine linen and purple is your covering.

My Mother Mary, interspersed with these items

about your good housekeeping, there are others that show you are a good business woman as well:

You are like a merchant's ship, bringing your bread from afar, you have tasted and seen that your traffic is good; you have made fine linen and sold it, and delivered a girdle to the Chanaanite.

O Mary, if you did all this, perhaps there *was* need of angels to help you with the lesser details! On the other hand, I prefer to think that you really did accomplish all this and in addition had much time for prayer — the kind of prayer and meditation that had been taught you in the Temple, and had been deepened and strengthened by the Holy Spirit.

Really, Mary, there are many counterparts of such a combination of business woman and housewife in the present economic situation. It is comforting that the women of today can take example from you in very practical ways, so that it can be prophesied of them as of you:

"She shall laugh in the latter day." That perhaps is the explanation of that problem of mine about the contrast between your speech while you were on earth, and your words when you appeared to your special children in the "latter days." Your children do indeed rise up and call you blessed.

In the simple details of your housekeeping, Mary, I like to think of you sewing, cleaning, cooking, washing. It's what we do today. Discounting the differences in the matter of electrification: iceboxes, illumination, dishwashers, polishers, sewing machines, and most other household gadgets, it's what women of today do. You went to the well for water, so you probably appreciated water more than we do now. Perhaps that's why wells and springs appear as one result of your apparitions. We, too, though, have to conserve water in times of drought. You washed clothing in the running stream rather than turning on your washing machine and listening to the radio while the swishing, automatic paddles did the work. For light, we merely touch a button, while you took much more time and effort in cleaning a lamp, filling it with oil, arranging the wick properly.

Your growing Son, Mary, must have been keenly observant of all your household activities. He spoke later of the silliness of hiding a light under a bushel instead of putting it where it would light the room. To your Son was applied that prophecy of Isaias (42:3) that He would not quench the smoking flax; and that didn't make much sense to me until I learned that the fibres of flax were twisted to form a wick for candle or lamp. He must have watched you, Mary, as you nursed into flame the smouldering bits of fiber. He must have seen how discouraging it was if a careless draft should extinguish the flame before it came to full strength.

Whether you were actually destitute (as some have suggested), or merely not wasteful, should you have lost a coin, He must have watched you or helped you sweep diligently until you found it. He spoke of a house that had been "swept and garnished." He knew from you the process of leavening a mass of sodden dough with yeast.

And the food? Perhaps He had in mind your simplicity and efficiency when He said to Martha: "Don't bother about so much fuss and frills — just a simple dish is needed." Perhaps Martha wanted to make sure there was parsley sprinkled over the potatoes, mushroom gravy for the meat, and some specially attractive device for salad and dessert.

Martha got all hot and bothered, and took it out on her sister Mary, who sat and seemingly did nothing! Mary, my Mother, you didn't get all hot and bothered except perhaps that one time when Jesus remained in Jerusalem and His place was hidden from you. *That* was certainly something to get all hot and bothered about!

There are other reflections of your housekeeping in the speech of Jesus: homey things like hens, lilies, sparrows; new cloth as useless to patch old garments, or old bottles for new wine; country things like crops and fishing. If you were also that counterpart of the valiant woman — a business woman — He knew about it and thought of it in such parables as the unjust steward, or the merchant dealing in pearls, or the talents: "Trade until I come." It's a queer thing, Mary — He was a carpenter and the son of a carpenter, but there is nothing in His parables or examples about such occupational things as the making of chairs, benches, tables, cabinets. Building, yes: the building of a tower, or the building of a house on sand — but in this He was more concerned with the foundation, or with the business aspect.

My own home life, sweet Mother, was simple and unpretentious as homes go these days. Perhaps it can be said of the majority of religious: we come from homes where father, mother, and children are united in bonds of common interest, common education, common economic situations.

The date of my entrance into your own religious household, Mary, was January fifteenth. I was so pleased to note recently that it is the feast of "Blessed Virgin Mary of Prompt Succour." I suppose your succour for me on this occasion was "prompt," though I must take it on faith, for the fulfillment of my vocation was a long-drawn-out affair of discouragements and frustrations and obstacles. However, when time is looked at in the light of eternity, I imagine it will turn out to have been "prompt" in His sense of the word — prompt in the sense that it came exactly when it was needed.

My mother was forty-four years old when I entered, Mary — probably your own age at the time Jesus left you. She left me in the convent parlor, giving a long backward look at my postulant dress with its unaccustomed full, long skirt, the veiled frame of a cap atop my curly hair pulled back in unaccustomed primness.

The Gospel for this January fifteenth feast is, appropriately, the story of the miracle at Cana — when His hour came suddenly because of your "prompt succour" — and the Offertory begs: "Remember O Virgin Mary, as you stand in the sight of God, that you speak good things for us and turn away His anger from us." But then, sweet Mother, it is renowned that "your love is no wise unmindful of those who remember you."

O Mary, Queen of good housekeepers, pray for us!

The feast of your espousals comes on the twenty-third. Another of the murals in the sanctuary of St. Ann's church, Mother, is the picture of your betrothal to St. Joseph. Looming in the background is the Temple (more Greek than Hebrew in its architecture, but the artist was not concerned with authentic details). Before the Temple on a sort of plaza stands the High Priest in garments prescribed by Moses, blessing the united hands of a not-too-aged St. Joseph and you — a little girl, veiled now and lately released from the Temple school. St. Joseph is holding your right hand with his, and in his left he holds the blossoming rod which tradition tells us furnished the sign that he was to be chosen as your spouse. To the left of the group, and somewhat apart, there stands a young man in very tight clothing, breaking a blossomless rod across his knee. He is evidently a rejected suitor, Mary, and his face has such an expression of fury! I used to look long at that picture — actually the rod-breaking young man with its suggestion of violence attracted my attention more than the dignified group, and I felt sorry for him. But I thought, too, if he were capable of such a temper, maybe he wouldn't have been tolerant and patient and obedient as St. Joseph turned out to be.

But you gave your hand to Joseph, Mary, and you gave your trust to him, and whether or not you confided to him the knowledge of your vow of virginity, he protected you and sheltered you; he let you go on that journey to Elizabeth; and after the angel's message to him what care, what tenderness, what love and reverent fear he must have felt toward you!

So, since this special month, my Mother, is devoted to the Holy Family as well as to the Infancy of Jesus, in union with you I shall spend two very special days — family days. First I shall come with you on what I imagine would be the ordinary routine of your life — not that any one day in your grace-filled existence could be really ordinary.

You rise, Mary — no doubt early, for there are things to be done; and in the early dawn you clothe yourself in your daytime garments, raising your mind and heart to God your Father in thanks for the new day that is beginning. There is fire to be kindled from the wood your Son brought in the night before. There is breakfast to be prepared. I don't doubt you were a good cook, Mary, for surely everything you did was done with what we call "perfection of ordinary actions." The food? Perhaps cakes of meal fried in oil, perhaps hot milk if it was a chilly morning.

Then, after Jesus and Joseph had left for the shop, it wasn't too much trouble to clear away the dishes and put the cottage in order. There were sick to be visited in the village; some neighbor may have asked you to stop in to give her some advice, to listen to her tale of woe. You stopped at the well for water, and as you drew up the brimming vessel, the children flocked about you — they had been watching for you. They wanted a story, they wanted you to play with them. But you told them to come to you after lunch, for the morning was getting on, your men folk would be in for the noon meal — a meal of fruit, perhaps, and milk and bread.

When the children came to you in the afternoon, you went out with them in the sunshine. You taught them the little songs you had learned in your Temple days, you chanted with them the praise of God, you told them the story they had asked for: a story of Jesus in His boyhood days. You sent them down along the street as the shadows lengthened. There was a little sewing to be done while the light lasted, and the evening meal to be prepared. Darkness came, and you lighted candles. Your family returned and washed up at the doorway where you had set basins of fresh water for them.

In Elizabeth's home, there would have been servants to do this for them; there would have been precious ointments to soothe their toil-roughened, splinter-scarred hands. But you served them out of your poverty, Mary; and when they entered, you had the table neatly set, the candles burning, the food appetizing. How flattering the candle-light upon your pure and perfect features! How it high-lighted the lovely face of your Boy! How it pointed up the furrows, the wrinkles, the whitened beard of your husband!

Joseph was silent. The day had brought disappointment: there was a patron who had not paid as he promised. The proper kind of wood was hard to get — the tools he had would not obey his strong hands. But he wasn't despondent. Only his shoulders seemed to droop more noticeably, his silence was deeper, his manner ever more gentle. You worried a little, Mother, because his appetite was not hearty, and you urged him to eat.

But Jesus ate heartily. His eyes twinkled into yours as He passed His plate for more — and yet more. Oh, this was the best part of the day! You three lingered over it — Jesus talked of their work, Joseph's burden lightened, you told them of the children you had taught, and of the sick women you had visited, or of the neighbors you had counseled.

Jesus helped you put away the fragments of the meal, wash the wooden bowls, set everything in order. There were long, sweet hours of prayer — prayer that scarcely differed from the homely conversation that had gone before. The Psalms of David were chanted, the house blessing invoked. Then the fire was banked, and it was bedtime.

The long, dreamless hours of sleep gave you strength and peace and renewed gratitude for the peace and security.

So now come with me during my day, Mary. I rise at the sound of the bell and answer "Amen" to the bell ringer's "Lord Jesus, preserve us in peace." I switch on the light at my bedside, and close the window if the

weather is chilly. But if the air is really cold, the heat
is singing up from the radiator and our cell is comfortable enough to dress in. I make my Morning Offering
and recall the subject of meditation — and my resolu-
tion to spend this day with you, Mary, however different from yours it might be in outward circumstances.
Perhaps I have over-simplified your day; perhaps the
items in my day are not so complex as they sometimes
seem — but both days are yours, Mary.

When dressed, I join the groups moving chapel-
ward. There is the usual situation in regard to the
ventilation: someone opens a door very softly so as to
get more circulation of air without attracting the notice
of the draft-fearing ones. Someone drapes a shawl over
her head and looks balefully at an open window. We
settle down to meditation. All those bowed heads, all
those reverent bodies: surely, Mary, there is a great
upsweep of love and worship for your Son during this
half hour!

Then Mass, with its hymns and union with the Priest
in responses — Holy Communion — thanksgiving — the
Morning Office. The "Little Hours" seem very long
indeed for human bodies weary after twelve hours' fast
(even though seven of them were spent in sleep) and
two hours of prayer.

Breakfast — this morning we had batter cakes that
perhaps were not so different from the kind of breakfast you had; though I dare say we are more vitamin-
and-calorie conscious.

Then a hurry-scurry rush to get domestic "charges"
cleaned, beds made, cells put in order, in time to greet
the children as they arrive. We teach our children
what we learned from you, Mother, and from the Holy
Spirit, from our own school days, from summer schools,

extension courses, ardent application to study — and from experience.

The children are not always easy to handle — these somewhat unrestrained youths of today, but they are frank, honest, and amenable to correction. We love them, and our hearts expand with the knowledge that they love us and look to us for guidance. We are glad when recess comes, or lunch time — glad for their sakes as well as ours!

Lunchtime fortifies us both physically and mentally, so that we return to the classroom (after a not-too-hurried visit to the Blessed Sacrament) with renewed energy to battle with ignorance, waywardness, and restlessness. Then comes the welcome dismissal bell. We shepherd our children into coats, snowsuits, gloves, boots perhaps — so much impedimenta — and get them to their various buses and machines.

It's the parents' turn now, and we wave them good-bye with a sense of achievement: one more day gone, another to be prepared for. But first we have a brisk walk in the sunshine, or perhaps we visit the sick, or have a conference with some worried parent. We make a wistful visit to the community room, in case "party" (cookies, candy, fruit) has been left out for us — and generally it has been.

So it's prayer time again: spiritual reading and evening office when we join you again, Mary, in David's psalms of praise and supplication. Supper, study, recreation with a chance of sewing or fancy work, or maybe music and games if it is a special feast. Then night prayers, blessed night prayers, when we invoke God's blessing on our house, and unite ourselves to you in the petitions: House of Gold, Ark of the Covenant,

Mirror of Justice, etc., pray for us! Examination of conscience, meditation prepared for the next day.

And so to bed! Mary, Patron of home, daily routine, patron of family life whether within a religious community or within a private home, pray for us!

Anent family unitedness, Mary, our superior is very much like you: she likes "regular observance" because it brings us all together. And she herself is the most regular of observance. But she is like you in other things, too: toward the sick she is so kind and thoughtful that one would think she had nothing else to do except provide for their welfare; yet she is accessible to the well, too; especially accessible to those with problems or sorrow. She loves little things: young animals or babies. Our "hundredfold" is very obvious when we have such a one to govern us, sweet Mother — and it's easy to rely on the Divine Providence of God which she represents! Thank you for her; please thank your Son for her, and should the next Superior be not so satisfactory — well, take care of that, too, for us!

By the way, St. Joseph is a very silent element in my life, too, Mary. Our Lady, Spouse of the silent St. Joseph, pray for me. And because I have endowed you with so many titles, apropos or not, perhaps this is a good place to append the article on your titles:

2. OUR LADY OF MANY TITLES

Some of her titles have to do with the names of places where Our Lady appeared: like Fatima, Lourdes, La-Salette, Guadalupe, or Walsingham. And while we are honoring her with geographical titles, we might also call her Our Lady of Nazareth, or Bethlehem, of Egypt, Jerusalem, of Cana in Galilee, and of Calvary.

A few of her titles have reference to various devo-
tions to her; for example: Our Lady of the Rosary, Our
Lady of the Scapular, Our Lady of the Miraculous
Medal.

Some are figurative, poetic, and refer to the prophecies of her, such as: Tower of Ivory, House of Gold,
Seat of Wisdom, Root of Jesse.

But many of them, and the dearest of them, refer to
her personal qualities; and these we might know from
the study of her life, though there is tantalizingly little
told about her in the Gospels — in three instances she
is merely mentioned:

"Thy mother and thy brethren stand without,"

"There stood by the cross Mary, His Mother,"

"They persevered in prayer with Mary, the mother
of Jesus."

Then there are four incidents that are given in more
detail: the annunciation and the subsequent visit to
Elizabeth; the journey to Bethlehem, the birth of
Christ, the visits of shepherds and Magi, with the subsequent flight into Egypt; the loss in the temple; the
miracle at Cana.

It is as though the Holy Spirit said:

"These are just samples of what My spouse is. All
through the ages, there will be more manifestations;
but they will be developments of the original pattern,
and of the same texture as these brief revelations."

For these seven "samples" epitomize the whole of
our Lady's characteristics, and furnish the pattern of
perfect life to all who would imitate her.

St. Gabriel initiates us into knowledge of her by his
litany of praise:

"Hail, full of grace!"

She was Virgin most Prudent when she trembled at

his salutation and when after his prophecy, she asked:
"How shall this be done, because I know not man?"

But after the Angel's explanation, her ready submission "Behold the handmaid of the Lord" proclaimed her as Virgin most Obedient, Virgin most Fruitful.

When those little-girl sandals trod the hillside with sturdy surety, in her haste to help her cousin Elizabeth, she was Virgin most Zealous, Model of Guests.

Elizabeth followed Gabriel in her litany of praise:
"Blessed art thou among women! Whence is this to me that the mother of my Lord should come?" and the Blessed Virgin became Mary of the Magnificat, Mary student of Scripture, Mary divinely inspired, in her response:
"My soul doth magnify the Lord."

Spouse of the Holy Ghost is her title for those seeking inspiration and guidance, for "when as His mother Mary was espoused to Joseph, before they came together she was found with child of the Holy Ghost."

Joseph, all unaware of the miraculous conception, and troubled at his most certain observation of her pregnancy, was minded to put her away privately. Then did Mary become Martyr of misunderstanding, Mary most meek Virgin and most silent.

The Angel revealed to Joseph the Holy Spirit's intervention and promised: "She shall bring forth a son, and thou shalt call his name Jesus, for he shall save his people from their sins."

Then Joseph joined Gabriel and Elizabeth in his praise of her: "Mother of the Saviour, refuge of sinners, Mary, Mother of God."

In that journey to Bethlehem for enrollment under an earthly power, she was Mary of Obedience, Mary of humble submission, Mary of patience.

"And it came to pass . . . that she brought forth her first-born son, wrapped him in swaddling clothes, and laid him in a manger." Then was she Mary of simplicity, Mary patron and model of all young mothers.

At the hasty visit of the shepherds, and the more ceremonial visit from the Magi, she was Mary Queen of hostesses. But when she kept all these things in her heart, pondering over them, she was virgin most prudent, patron of those who love the interior life.

At the presentation of Jesus in the Temple, Simeon and Anna joined Gabriel, Elizabeth, Joseph, the shepherds, and the Magi in their praise of her; and she became Mary obedient to the law — but also, at Simeon's prophecy, Mary of the sword-pierced heart.

When, as a result of the Magi's visit, they were bidden to fly into Egypt, then was she again virgin most prudent, virgin of confiding obedience, patron of exiles.

Later, the three-day loss in the Temple intruded upon the peaceful years of security at Nazareth, and she became Mary patron of lost children, Mary comfort of sorrowing mothers deprived of their little ones.

But when "He went down with them, and came to Nazareth, and was subject to them," she continued her role of Model of housekeepers, Queen of an orderly household.

At the marriage feast in Cana of Galilee, she was again the model of guests, the compassionate patron of hosts in her appeal: "They have no wine." And when she said to the waiters: "Whatsoever He shall say to you, do," she was Our Lady of Good Counsel, refuge of the doubtful, recourse for those in need.

"Blessed is the womb that bore thee, and the breast that nourished thee" was the praise of the woman in the crowd of His hearers, and Jesus proclaimed Himself

among the increasing number of Mary's devotees, when
He replied:

"Yes, blessed are those (My mother chief among
them) who hear the word of God and keep it."

Blessed but most sorrowing above all women was
she when she stood by the cross of Jesus and heard herself bequeathed to John. Thus was summarized her
life of abandonment, detachment, and burning devotion to the will of God. Thus she exemplified her complete role:

Daughter of the Eternal Father,
Spouse of the Holy Ghost,
Mother of the Redeemer,
Queen of the Infant Church (oh, fortunate for us!)
Refuge of sinners.

Like the members of the early Church, may we too
persevere in prayer with Mary, the Mother of Jesus,
Our Lady of Perseverance!

3. OUR LADY OF SILENCE

Because Jesus is the Word,
    Mary is the silence.
The potent Word cannot be heard
    Save in surrendering silence.
Our Lady of Silence kept words in her heart,
Our Lady had chosen the better part.
    But silence fructified in speech
    When the Holy Spirit began to teach:
Then she spoke her fleeting
Answer to the Angel's greeting,
    To Elizabeth she chanted
    That her prayer at last was granted;
There was a cry of protest, woe, and pity
After her search for Jesus in the Holy City;
    To her Son she came to plead
    At Cana, for the bridegroom's need.
Our Lady of Silence utters words of power
That through succeeding generations flower
    Forth in song
    Echoing to prolong
The love of those who call her blest
Because the Word responds at her behest.

VI

1. FEBRUARY

This month, Mother mine, we begin by celebrating
the feast of one who must have been a favorite son of
yours: St. Ignatius, Bishop and martyr, who is famous
for proclaiming:

"I am Christ's wheat, let me be milled by the teeth
of the beasts that I may become spotless bread." That
recalls our Saviour's remark about the necessity for the
grain of wheat to die before it can bear fruit. It
brings us in adoration to the thought of the Blessed
Sacrament, the "wheat of the elect."

But it also foreshadows the prophecy of Simeon that
will be quoted on the morrow: that through the sword
of sorrow you also, Mary, will be ground, shredded,
rent with grief. Yet on the whole, it is a joyous feast.
Your Purification, Mary, the Presentation of your Son
in the Temple and (liturgically) the blessing of candles
make it a three-fold solemnity.

Much has been made of your fulfilling the law even
though technically you were not bound by it. But it
all seems in accordance with your simplicity. Our
Lord was to say afterward that not one jot or tittle of
the law would pass away before it be fulfilled: a jot
— or an "i" which is the simplest of letters — pointing
upward, with its dot or "tittle" like a tiny star above
it. It's like you, Mary, and I'm sure you were saying
in your heart the "i" that is I must decrease that He
might increase.

The gorgeous panoply that the Second affords us, Mary, gives us the blessings of the candles all intermingled with the spirit of the feast:

"Lord, . . . who by Thy command didst cause this liquid to come by the labour of bees to the perfection of wax, and didst on this day fulfill the petition of the just man Simeon, we beseech thee . . . by the intercession of Blessed Mary ever Virgin, whose festival is this day devoutly celebrated . . . that Thou wouldst vouchsafe to bless and sanctify these candles for the use of men, and for the health of bodies and souls." Each prayer re-echoes that three-fold theme: light, purification, and the buying back of the forty-day-old Infant.

We join, Mary, in spirit we join in the procession that occurs between the blessing and the distribution of candles and the beginning of Mass. Simeon is your cross-bearer on this occasion, then Anna with her zeal that all might recognize the Light of the World; then angels: angels of the Nativity — Gabriel, and that "Angel of the Testament" whom Malachy mentions: "Behold I send my Angel and he shall prepare the way before My face; and presently the Lord whom you seek, and the Angel of the Testament whom you desire, shall come to the Temple." That "Angel to prepare the way" might be St. John Baptist, sweet Mary, so we'll admit him; and since he's only ten months old at this time, we'll have Elizabeth in the procession, too.

My procession is going to be quite long, Mary, for I've put into it all the people I pray for in the Mementos of the Mass: my Superiors; those in temptation, doubt, despair; the souls of beloved ones who have gone before me; then all those who represent your Son's Church: priests, my own missionary Bishop, mothers, toiling fathers, teachers, housewives, lovers, the aged, the crippled. "Procedamus in Pace," says the deacon.

Then all proceed with lighted candles (and may it be in peace), forming an advance guard for: Joseph carrying his basket of turtle doves, and you, my Mother, carrying the Light of the World: "Because the mystery of the Word made flesh, the light of His glory, hath shone anew upon the eyes of our mind; that while we acknowledge Him to be God seen by men, we may be drawn by Him (the Latin word is *rapiamur,* which suggests a far stronger force than mere drawing!) to the love of things unseen."

The French painter Bourdon has a picture of your Presentation, Mother, which does not seem so orderly or dignified as the Gospel narrative, or as the procession I have just imagined. In his picture, the High Priest is in the shadow, his great book lighted only by one candle. He seems to be droning along with whatever words are required for the Purification or for the Presentation; but you and Simeon are paying no attention to him: the light is focused on your white headcovering, on Simeon's beautiful beard. It is made to shine still more strongly on the baby Jesus whom you are handing over to Simeon — not quite so carefully as one would expect in the handling of so young a baby, for the little dimpled arm is dangling unsupported below your wrist. Below, crouched in a rather abandoned position is — presumably — another mother, with a somewhat older child leaning against her shoulder. If she is waiting her turn for the Purification, she must have put it off considerably longer than forty days; and certainly, from her bodily position, one might say she feels at home and informal in her Father's house!

This picture is no doubt full of merit, my Mother, so

far as art is concerned, but it fills one with pity to
note that the artist is a non-Catholic. It is one of
those selected by Cynthia Pearl Maus in her *The
World's Greatest Madonnas,* and while she has done a
good work in going to authentic sources (except for
the Scripture quotations, which are from King James'
version) there is one exasperating thing about it: much
as she mentions you, Mary, she never uses the word
"blessed." Now, why should she avoid your prerogative? She'll say "the Mother of Jesus"; she talks about
the Council of Ephesus that proclaimed you the Mother
of God; but always there is mention merely of "the
Virgin," or "the Virgin Mary." Do something about
her, will you, sweet Mary? She must have learned great
devotion to you in the process of her learned compila-
tion. Now — H.M. Gillette came into the Church in
a hurry before he had gotten very far in the study of
your shrines. Make a lot of people study your shrines,
will you, my Mother?

There is a more romanticized picture of you, Mother,
painted by the Englishman Frederick Goodall. Here
your face is lovely indeed, your posture graceful, and
it is you who are holding to your breast the turtle doves;
but (like the Greeks in the time of your Son's public
life) "we want to see Jesus!"

You are about fifteen years old at this time, Mary,
and it is amazing that the artists picture you as much
older. Maybe it is the clothing, though, that makes
you look older — those sweeping Greek tunics and
cloaks and veils. The girls of today, with their shorts
and jeans — or even with their more modest and simple
cotton dresses, look much, much younger to us. O
Lady of the Purification, protect the youth of today
in the face of prevailing immodest fashions of dressing!

Our school girls of the age of fifteen today have just come from the ordeal of examinations (in February, that is). They are starting a new semester this month with renewed hope (we hope!), for they have gotten back into routine upset by the Christmas holidays. Unless Easter comes very early, they are facing a two-months' stretch of regular school work. They (as well as more mature persons) are getting tired if the winter seems long-drawn out. During February there comes just a hint of spring — enough to stir one's blood and make one fearful lest the buds should come out too soon and be destroyed by March's blizzards and bluster.

Do you know, Mary, it very seldom rains the whole day of any of your feasts? In fact, I don't ever remember a completely rainy feast day of yours. Alfred Barrett has a beautiful poem to you in which he hails you "Our Lady of the Weather":

Snow-maiden, Rainbow-maiden, Sun-gowned Queen
. . . Our Lady of the weather . . . through my soul
Four seasons roll, the weather of my own
    inconstancy."

But of course, according to the soul's need or fancy, you can be called Our Lady of everything, or everywhere, or (as I wrote for you) Our Lady of Many Titles.

It is under one of these many titles that we salute you on the eleventh: Our Lady of Lourdes. What a poetic affair that was! You appear in a grotto with your rosary which you motion to Bernadette to say with you. There is a rose at your feet, you raise your hands with a graceful gesture, then you look upon the child and smile. You tell her to dig until a spring of water bursts forth. It was a joyous thing, even though, Mary, you had to say to her:

"I do not promise to make you happy in this world, but in the next." Just the same, before those persecutions came, before the crowd came to make of the affair a jest and a sordid display, there were lovely, intimate moments. It is recorded, Mary, that you even laughed when Bernadette came with pen and paper for you to write your name and wishes. The greatest result of your shrine at Lourdes, Mary, refers back to that prayer in the blessing of candles: restored health of body *and soul*.

There are shrines for you all over the world, Mary. It is as though you want to make up through the centuries for the fact that your activity was so circumscribed during your life. There is a device I use for a sleepless night: to roam geographically around to your shrines: Our Lady of the Catacombs, Our Lady protectress of Rome, Our Lady of Einsiedeln in Switzerland (Our Lady of the Hermits), Our Lady of Walsingham in England, of Rocamadour on the Paris-Toulouse line in France, with its curious tradition of Zaccheus; of Oostacker near Ghent in Belgium, of LaSalette in south France, of Hal near Brussels, of Prouille which tradition tells us is the cradle of the rosary. Is there any country unblest with at least one vision of you, some favorite shrine, some statue beloved in the hearts and traditions of the people?

Yes. My heart says yes — there is: The United States has no miraculous shrine or miraculous picture, or authentic appearance of you. Why is this, Mary? Is it a subtle compliment — because really you *do* appear in places where there is much need of reform? We —

we have dedicated to you our country, and your shrine
in Washington is struggling toward completion. Bless
it, Mother of mine, won't you?

Shrines all over the world — but France, Italy, Spain,
and the Spanish-American countries seem more favored
than all the rest. Is it because they need it more? O
Mother, when it comes to a question of *need*, turn
thy eyes of pity to the Asiatic countries: to China,
Korea, and Japan!

There is an intriguing picture of you, painted by a
modern Japanese artist, Luke Hasegawa, called "Our
Lady of Japan." It is intriguing because of the wealth
of details: the wire fence surrounding a sort of compound from which you rise, a very black-haired Infant
in your arms, the high mountains beyond you, before
you a harbor with many ships, on the shore a variety
of small, flat-roofed homes, and on the road the suggestion of many, many persons coming toward you.
Our Lady of Japan, win hearts to you, that you may
present them to your Son!

The Chinese artist, Lu Hung-nien, has a painting of
you entitled the Madonna of the Lantern Festival.
Here again there are so many disparate details that one
might say: "Puzzle — find the lanterns." You are holding your Son, the Light of the world, who seems sleep-
ing, and you are looking down upon some very Chinese-
looking angels who are carrying, respectively: a candle,
a censer, a peculiar-looking fish with banners trailing
from it, a distorted bird with four-fold tail; and — yes,
there is a lantern: the artist has painted himself
sheltering behind your veil, and he carries what is at
last recognizable as a lantern. O blessed Lady of
China, pray for your Chinese children!

My geographic wanderings should have put me to

sleep long ago, O Our Lady of here, Our Lady of there, Our Lady of everywhere. Whether we have a miraculous shrine or picture or medal or whatever, you do go with us, sweet Mother, in our devotion, companion in our travels and occupations, Our Lady, pride of all our race, dear Patron of our every place!

The mention of your shrines and paintings brings to mind the fact that so many representations are crowded with symbols of you. The imagination delights in the great variety of your symbols: sun, moon, stars, lily, rose, a garden enclosed, a well, a fountain sealed up, a gate; the Cedar of Lebanon, a mirror, a sealed book, the bush which Moses saw unconsumed — besides those clouds that I mentioned, which nobody so far has done anything about — but I cherish my home-made title: "My Lady of the Clouds, pray for me — pray for those in doubt and indecision; pray for those in darkness who are seeking whether consciously or not the Light of the world."

All these symbols, Mary, having their own identity, may also be used allegorically to portray some trait or characteristic of yours. But if there is one oddity more puzzling than another in this modern world, it is the exasperating, dangerous and devil-inspired idea of translating *all* reality into symbolism of some kind. "Mother symbol" will be sufficient to dismiss your importance in this present world where people are trying to make complexes, ideologies, and abstractions take the place of holy (and responsibility-burdened) reality. "Sadist — or masochist" they say of one who preaches or practices the penance you asked for. "Father Complex" they say, when they hear the portrayal of our Heavenly Father as a real, personal God, Father, Provider; or when we speak of St. Joseph as the shadow of God the Father. They do not speak of individuals — they talk of humanity, or types; of social uplift instead of participation in the mystical body; of the Divinity instead of a personal God. And all this is the devil's device to minimize or destroy the value of the soul.

Meanwhile you, my sweet Mother, go your way — or the way of grace, crushing beneath your heel this very real trick of Satan's to get souls away from the idea of personal responsibility, from a recognition of the worth of the individual.

On the twenty-seventh (twenty-eighth in Leap Year) comes the feast of one who regarded all this complexity of symbolism as something very foolish. He regarded you as a very real person, real enough to make him give up a promising wordly career to follow you and serve you in the most penitential of orders: St. Gabriel of Our Lady of Sorrows, Passionist. He is rather a comforting saint, My Mother, for like the Little Flower he did nothing extraordinary, but simply and faithfully followed the vocation of total dedication to you and to God. He is the patron of youth, and especially of young Religious.

Appropriately, the twenty-seventh is also a feast for you under the title: "Our Lady of Light." Our Lady of Light in the light that shone round about the shepherds, our Lady of Light in the glimmering of Joseph's lantern, and later during the dark nights of Egypt; our Lady of Light in the little household at Nazareth, tending the lamps of early twilight; our Lady of Light in the Resurrection; our Lady of Light in your many appearances, especially at Fatima, shining like snow, transparent like crystal, your face luminous, causing the sun to dance while the stars and the moon stood in awe — oh, our beautiful Lady of Light, pray for us!

2. THREE FIRST-AID EXPERTS

The neighbor woman came for aid
And solace from the little maid
 Newly come to live next door
 In a house like hers, low-roofed and poor.
But the neighbor wept about the drains;
 The cow had broken from her shed;
The gaping holes let in the rains:
 "Go to Joseph," Mary said.

The Holy Child was nearly six,
He trotted to the shop with sticks:
 Joseph might lend nails and twine
 To make support for flowering vine.
But the hammer slipped, the nails cut deep,
 The little fingers throbbed and bled.
The little Boy began to weep:
 "Run to Mary," Joseph said.

The bride was sad at the wedding feast,
As the jars of wine too soon decreased.
 She looked around, her dark eyes wide
 With fear and shame, lest the guests deride.
But Mary sensed the bride's alarm;
 At her words, the worry fled:
Quietly, and with gentle charm,
 "I'll go to Jesus," Mary said.

VII

1. MARCH

This month, Mary, is such a variety of contrasts. It is likely to be a solemn, serious month for one reason: that most of it (sometimes all of it) is Lent. On the other hand, there are so many joyous feasts. It is dedicated to your faithful, loyal spouse, St. Joseph, "the shadow of the eternal Father."

I want to talk to you about Joseph, Mother. One can realize that the eternal Father picked him for the very reason that his own particular "flavor" would mirror the traits of the Father in Heaven. He was just — which as we know in Scripture means he had a perfect balance of virtue. He was silent — and *how* silent the Father in Heaven can be! Only once did He speak — from the clouds — "This is My beloved Son in whom I am well pleased. Hear ye Him." St. Joseph didn't even say that much, though he must have said it in his actions and in the whole plan of his life: "This is my foster Son. He has well pleased both Mary and me. Hear Him and you too will be well pleased in grace and peace and love."

He worked with his hands, Mary, and that usually produces peace and serenity in a man. I wonder if he whistled at his work, as do so many carpenters that I know of? My own silent father was not a carpenter by trade, but he belonged to the vast society of "fix-it-yourself" amateurs, and really there was nothing about the house that his clever hands could not fix. And he whistled when he worked, especially in sawing and whittling and joining.

Carpentry is considered a lowly occupation, Mary, but I cannot believe that the neighbors scorned your spouse. His trade was humble, but there's no reason to imagine that he was cheated of his pay, that he had to wrangle and argue and bargain. I'd rather think that friends and neighbors admired him, respected his work, and sought him often for his skill and reliability. There might have been more wonderment than contempt in their later exclamation:

"'Is not this the carpenter's Son?'"

Surely his workshop must have attracted children — who does not love a carpenter shop with its smell of wood shavings and glue, its eye-catching variety of tools and gadgets? One can fancy St. Joseph would mend toys for the little ones, or guide small hands in some piece of construction. He evidently taught Jesus to work with him, for later our Saviour was referred to as "the carpenter" as well as "the Son of the carpenter."

There is a legend, Mary, of an old, old Rabbi who had a precious manuscript — a great thesis written with much labor and research, that he wanted to preserve most fittingly in a special chest. The Rabbi himself is telling the story: how he went to a carpenter, giving exact specifications, the choice of the most durable and beautiful wood to be carved in exquisite pattern, the hinges and lock to be just so. As he tells it, his hearer is getting more and more eager to see this manuscript that required so valuable a case, but the Rabbi keeps talking about his acquaintance with the carpenter, and how the Rabbi's own philosophy changed as the construction of the chest progressed. He keeps stroking the wood, fingering the carving, the lock, and the hinges. Finally the hearer breaks in with "But the manuscript? Let me see it!" The Rabbi, opening the box, displays only emptiness — with the remark: "Oh — that — I burned it long ago. The importance of this box is that it was made by Christ, the son of Joseph — and Son of the Eternal God." Whether that story is true or not, Mary, it's the sort of thing that *could* have happened.

You know, my Mother, it is scarcely a matter of surprise that *you* are admired, loved, venerated all over the world, considering the many legends about you, considering the inspiration that you have been to painters and writers, considering your many apparitions and revelations, considering that you have proved again and again that you are the Refuge of sinners, the Mother of Mercy. The remarkable thing is that St. Joseph is so universally venerated! He has never appeared to anybody so far as is authentically known; his speech was never recorded either in Scripture or in private revelations; he never commanded: "Build me a Church here; paint me a picture." He is universally loved, but he is the saint of silence. He is the patron saint of the interior life, of family life, of happy marriages, and of a happy death. St. Teresa and many others committed to him their financial affairs. He gained all this veneration, Mary, because you wanted it that way, and because the Heavenly Father wanted it that way. I must say, though, that St. Joseph has certainly cooperated — in his silent way!

Now, I don't mean to intimate that you are particularly talkative, sweet Mary. You are the patron of silence in another way — in your own Mary-way. Because Jesus is the Word, you are the silence, for the potent Word could not be heard save in surrendered silence. You, our Lady of Silence, kept words in your heart. You were not heard except when you chanted your submission to the Angel, except when you intoned your answer to your cousin's welcome, except when you brought to Him, pleadingly, the need at Cana. When you do speak, you produce words so potent and wise that they go singing, leaping, echoing from generation to generation.

But you were silent: silent when you might have defended yourself against St. Joseph's suspicion; silent during your flight to Egypt and during the long, peaceful years of the Hidden Life. And beneath the Cross — O my Lady of Sorrow, what a deep, deep cloak of silence surrounded you then! Then if ever you might have asked: "My Son, why hast Thou done so to us?" But you were silent with the silence of submission, resignation — and perhaps (at last) of understanding.

During the month of March we may consider that practically the whole of your "Jesus life" is unfolded. Beginning with the age of fourteen when the angel appeared to you, on to the age of about twenty-six when Jesus was lost in the Temple, up to your age of forty-four when He left you to go about preaching — and finally to forty-eight when He hung upon the Cross.

O Mother! What a vast amount of grace, events, endurance, conjecture, meditation, research, instruction can be crammed into those thirty-four years of yours — all depicted within this month!

The twenty-fourth is the feast of your own special angel, Mary, and it is appropriate that it comes the day before your Day of days: the Annunciation. Hail, full of grace! How various and numerous have been the pictures inspired by that situation: "the angel Gabriel was sent from God into a city of Galilee, called Nazareth, to a virgin espoused to a man whose name was Joseph." What drama there is in the dialogue that followed!

Gabriel: Hail, full of grace, the Lord is with thee, blessed art thou among women.

Mary: (Silent — your whole attitude expresses deep thought, puzzlement; yes, and prudence. You look at the angel questioning, your face full of candor and innocence.)

Gabriel: (trying again) Fear not, Mary, for thou hast found grace with God. Behold, thou shalt conceive in thy womb, and shalt bring forth a son; and thou shalt call His name Jesus. . . .

Mary: (Continued silence — a silence of waiting. How could you *not* interrupt? But you don't speak, and the Angel goes on with further explanation, as though in further inducement.)

Gabriel: He shall be great and shall be called the Son of the most High, and the Lord God will give to Him the throne of David his father; and He shall reign in the house of Jacob forever, and of His kingdom there shall be no end.

Mary: (All that array of proof, all that appeal to prophecy, and you have only one practical question.) How shall this be done, because I know not man?

(Somehow, Mary, I think your final breaking of silence might be interpreted: "I know the prophecies — especially that made to Achaz that a virgin should conceive — but surely I cannot take it for granted that *I* am *that* virgin?" The angel confirms your supposition. He must be relieved that you finally spoke!)

Gabriel: The Holy Ghost shall come upon thee, and the power of the most High shall overshadow thee.

And therefore also the Holy which shall be born of thee shall be called the Son of God.

Mary: (Relaxed and peaceful in your silence. Gabriel feels that he has to bring you down to earth now, with a bit of what might be called family gossip; only it is meant as proof of the power of God — for you, who asked no proof.)

Gabriel: And behold, thy cousin Elizabeth, she also hath conceived a son in her old age; and this is the sixth month with her that is called barren, because no word shall be impossible with God.

Mary: (At long last saying the words for which heaven and earth were waiting.) Behold the hand-maid of the Lord, be it done unto me according to thy word.

The Italian artists have caught the beauty and drama of this scene, Mary, more than any of the others — not Angelico da Fiesole, though, so much as Titian. Fra Angelico painted you in the setting which he knew best: that of a monastery. There are those spaced columns, the vaulting arches, the fence shutting out the world beyond. It is of course great art, but I think the stylized figures, the angel's many-colored wings, the rather stiff pose he gives you, Mary, would not appeal to devotion so much as does Titian's picture. Titian places you in the marble court of a palace. You are kneeling, though the work basket beside you shows that you must have been sitting before Gabriel came. On the prie-dieu before you is an open book — presumably that of the prophets. And the angel! That virile figure of youthful beauty, clothed in garments that follow the lines of his graceful activity, his face alight with love and pleading, his uplifted right arm pointing to the dove that hovers as though awaiting your word, Mary, that He may descend upon you! It is, indeed, a most satisfying picture, and I am sure you must have loved your devoted artist; you must have inspired him with devotion long, long before he gained the skill to portray outwardly and so convincingly the inward vision that filled his soul with peace.

Maybe it sounds silly, Mary, to be describing your pictures to you — but why wouldn't I talk to you about the things that occupy my mind? I go into the chapel sometimes, and seeing a particularly lovely tribute to you on your altar, I'll say: "O Mary, you have roses today!" or "Sweet Mother, they've put on your altar the cloth I made for you" — as though you didn't know it anyway!

But you tell me things that I already know, too. You say to me as to the waiters at Cana: "Whatsoever He shall say to you, do it!" To me, as well as to the children of Fatima, you say: "Do penance, pray!" You tell me as well as all your other children: "Pray much and make sacrifices for sinners! Many souls go to hell because there are none to make sacrifices and pray for them."

The end of March is often sad, Mother, Mother of Sorrows, that is why I have written this study of you and the seven words your Son spoke from the Cross. And then, too, there is my idea of your first Way of the Cross — backwards — from the tomb all the long sad way to your home in the Cenacle.

2. MARY AND THE SEVEN WORDS

All her life, Mary went to the School of Theology. Her training began in the Temple, back in her little-girl days. Gabriel's salutation prepared her for matriculation in the liberal arts of divinity:

"The Holy Ghost shall come upon thee, and the power of the most High shall overshadow thee."

Like the earnest student she was, Mary kept all these words in her heart. Further progress was made when Simeon told her of her Son's destiny: "This child is set for the fall and resurrection of many in Israel." And then he foretold that her own heart would be pierced as with a sword. Again, losing her Child in Jerusalem and finding Him in the midst of the Doctors, she proceeded even more deeply into her study on the ways of God.

It was on Calvary that she received her final degree: Doctor of Holiness, Doctor of the Incarnate Word. Seven lectures formed that last supreme course, correlating her own precious recitations, preparing her for her position as Queen of the Apostles, of preachers, of teachers.

When she sang her song of songs in answer to Elizabeth's greeting, she made much of it like a summary of the inspired words she had long been pondering in her heart:

"My soul doth magnify the Lord," she exulted, obeying the Psalmist's exhortation: "O magnify the Lord with me, and let us extol his name." She proclaimed: "My spirit hath rejoiced in God my Saviour," for He had told her by the words of Ecclesiasticus: "For my spirit is sweet above honey and my inheritance above honey and the honeycomb . . . my memory is unto everlasting generations," and she emphasized this in her own words: "For behold from henceforth all generations shall call me blessed." And again: "His mercy from generation is unto generation." Taught by Isaiah's prayer: "Arise, put on strength, O thou arm of the Lord" she could assure her listeners: "He hath showed might in His arm." The words that followed: "He hath scattered the proud in the conceit of their heart, he hath put down the mighty from their seat and hath exalted the humble" had been taught her by her ancestor David: "The Lord bringeth to naught the counsels of the nations; and he rejecteth the devices of people, and casteth away the counsels of princes." Mary continues: "He hath filled the hungry with good things; and the rich he hath sent empty away," just as Anna, eleven centuries earlier, had sung: "They that were full before have hired themselves out for bread, and the hungry are filled . . . the Lord maketh poor and maketh rich; He humbleth and He exalteth."

Just as she integrated her Magnificat with the Scriptures, so Her Son was keeping in His heart the words of inspiration, until, at the high point of His agony, they burst forth in the words of the Twenty-first Psalm:

"My God, my God, why hast thou forsaken me!" There were many on Calvary who, had they not been blinded by hate, could have recited that Psalm with Him:

"Why hast thou forsaken me? . . . I am a worm and no man, the reproach of men, and the outcast of the people. All they that saw me have laughed me to scorn . . . for tribulation is very near. . . . I am poured out like water, and all my bones are scattered . . . they have numbered all my bones . . . they have looked and stared upon me. They parted my garments among them and upon my vesture they cast lots."

Surely, except that the High Priests deliberately shut their minds, the circumstances on Calvary must have recalled to them many verses of the Sixty-eighth Psalm: "Save me, O God, for the waters are come in even unto my soul . . . my enemies have grown strong who have

wrongfully persecuted me . . . they that sat in the gate
spoke against me . . . but as for me, my prayer is to
thee, O Lord . . . and I looked for one that would
grieve together with me, but there was none . . . and
they gave me gall for my food, and in my thirst they
gave me vinegar to drink."

Mary was grieving together with Him, but her suffering probably increased His own. When He cried
out "I thirst!" her memory went back to the time she
had said to Him: "Son, they have no wine," and even
though His hour had not then come, He supplied the
guests at the wedding feast by a miracle. In order to
quench the people's thirst, God gave to Moses the
power to bring water from the rock in the desert; but
when He Himself, blood-drained, fever-ridden, is so
sorely athirst that it is the only complaint of his physical sufferings that He makes on the cross, there is only
a dirty sponge filled with vinegar raised to His lips.
How fittingly He might have said then, as He once said
to the Samaritan woman: "If thou didst know the gift
of God, and who he is that saith to thee 'give me to
drink,' thou perhaps wouldst have asked of him, and
he would have given thee living water." Perhaps Mary
was recalling these words, and begging Him silently
to pour out the living water of grace.

When He cried out: "Father, forgive them, for they
know not what they do," she remembered His instruction: "He who has been forgiven more, hath the greater
love." Such was His appeal still for love — but to her
had been remitted the whole debt of the human race,
since she was free from the burden of original sin.
How her heart must have overflowed with love! And
how, too, she must have recalled her answer to the
angel: "How can this be, for I know not man!" It was

in a double sense that she knew him not, since no man had violated her virginity, and since she knew not how mankind could violate the infinite mercy of God by his ingratitude and wilful turning from Him.

The cry of Jesus: "My God, my God, why hast thou forsaken me?" recalled the scene in the Temple, when, in her joy at finding Him, she had asked: "My son, my son, why hast thou done so to us?" She knows now that this is the culmination of "His Father's business" — the supreme sacrifice.

At His magnificent promise to the Good Thief: "This day thou shalt be with Me in Paradise," she rejoiced that here at least was one fruit of His agony, and she whispered in sympathy with the forgiven criminal: "He that is mighty hath done great things for me, too."

When His ordeal was drawing to a close, and His weary head dropped upon His chest with the words: "It is consummated," she, too, could re-echo the consummation of her complete surrender to God, with the same words she used at the beginning: "My soul doth magnify the Lord." And at His final surrender: "Father, into thy hands I commend My spirit," she could well repeat: "He hath received Israel his servant, being mindful of his mercy."

In His special address to her: "Woman, behold thy son," she replied in full accord with His will: "Behold the handmaid of the Lord; be it done unto me according to thy word."

So, as she stood at the foot of the cross, she received the Mystical Body, the new-born Church, within her arms, wrapped it in the swaddling bands of her love, and placed it in the manger of her zeal.

Shepherds and kings would come to worship, glory and honor and magnificence would increase as the

years flowed by; but when Mary turned from the tomb
to go back to the Cenacle, it was the first of many processions from the shadow of sorrow and death to the
safe refuge of the Eucharistic dwelling place.

3. MARY'S WAY OF THE CROSS

The first Way of the Cross was made by Christ from
Jerusalem to Calvary. The second Way was retraced
in reverse by Mary — from Calvary to Jerusalem.

She, the Mother of fair Love, supervises the burial
rites of the Hope of Israel, thus completing the cycle
begun thirty-three years before:

> . . . she who felt Him moving in her womb
> Who wrapped and laid Him in a manger once
> Is still His handmaid, ready once again
> To wrap Him up and lay Him in His tomb[1]

She, the Comforter of the Afflicted, goes back to the
spot where Joseph had taken Him down from the cross.
Here she had washed away the clotted blood and dust
and spittle. The priests had withdrawn and left her
there:

> Now Caiphas is happy; he has won;
> He does not heed the frightened crows that run;
> Jerusalem is shaken, shock on shock
> Upheave the Temple sanctum, rive the rock;
> Now you may have the Thing that was your Son.

---

[1] This quotation, and those that follow, are taken from Father
Wm. A. Donaghy's sonnet series: *Stations of the Cross* published in
Spirit March, 1943.

She looks up at the cross, where once hung the Light of the world, the cross denuded now, blood-stained, with the lurid light of the sunless sky shining through the gaping holes where the nails had fastened His hands and feet. Three hours she had stood there, suffering in mind and soul all that was inflicted on the Body of the Holy One of Israel:

Once more He shifts on dislocated hips,
And cries aloud; His last vein bursts and drips —
He hangs upon His wooden monstrance, dead.

In her spirit re-echoes the sound of the blows that fastened Him there:

This sound had echoed back in Nazareth,
The thudding hammer on the singing nails,
And at each jolt she dies a double death.

A little further on: here is the spot where they had stripped Him. Before they put to death the Author of life, they had deprived Him of the last earthly possession — the seamless garment which she, the Cause of our Joy, had woven for Him:

Rough hands rip off the robe which has no seams,
And from reopened wounds the tired blood streams;
He stands among them, without word or will,
A shorn lamb, naked on this stunted hill.

A few feet down the Hill: this is where He fell that third time, fell so prostrate that the soldiers dragged Him up with ropes, and cursed the Cyrenean who had let the cross crash down upon Him, increasing the danger that He might die before He reached the place of execution. But . . .

> Upon this very road will Godfrey spur,
> Leading his knights — a charge of flaming swords
> Against the foemen of the Carpenter
> Who is King of Kings and Lord of Lords . . .

Then here — ah! here is the blessed spot where He had comforted the holy women of Jerusalem. He told them not to weep, He was the Good Shepherd; though seemingly the most abject of men, He showed Himself the Comforter of the Afflicted. For even then His heart was weeping that in the days to come the sons of these compassionate women would be subjected to humiliation, defeat, and slavery:

> And all His followers have disappeared
> Except these wailing women, jostled, jeered,
> Unwavering still, like her who sought the groat,
> And loyal yet, while priests and people gloat —
> This is a day of shame for brawn and beard.

There, at the foot of the hill, He had His second fall — stumbling and groping where the path began to ascend. All Simon's fresh strength had not availed to hold Him up and support also the cross:

> It is too much! His watery sinews yield,
> He sags and slumps; the wavering cross goes down;
> Gethsemane, the night, the lash, the crown —
> Could one poor heart bear these, though triple
>   steeled?

Perhaps that second fall was occasioned by the malice of the soldiers who saw that their Victim could so far forget His own plight as to stop and talk to Veronica, to accept the veil she handed Him, and to print upon the privileged cloth His own tortured features. Mary dwells lovingly on this spot. How she loved brave Veronica for doing what she herself would so gladly have done!

> The Temple veil hangs sundered into shreds,
> But still her tiny veil survives, unfurled,
> A banner and a bandage for the world.

Further on, within the wall of the town, is the place where they intercepted Simon the Cyrenean, returning from the country with a spade and basket, his two small frightened sons clinging to him:

> He burns the Romans with a look of hate,
> Then lends his grudging thews to this doomed
>   man . . .
> And from the Stranger, down the Cross's length
> There flow to Simon peace and tranquil strength.

Just within the gate is the sacred place so deeply impressed upon the heart of Nature that (according to tradition) the stone retained the impress of Mary's feet where she stood and strained to get a glimpse of Him. This is the spot where their pathways joined: she hastening from the Cenacle, He having come his painful way down the street from the Judgement Seat of Pilate.

Perhaps she thinks of Naim — of all the land
Where wonders blossomed as He walked three years;
Of Jairus, Lazarus, the withered hand,
Of flowing mercies and of drying tears;
And still she knows her bitter place and part —
He will not heal her withered, widowed heart.

John is supporting her now — they come to the place where the jolt of the cross had felled Him with its unguided, unwarned-of weight dropped upon His shoulders, He, the Lion of Juda — yet

From this mob a swelling, bestial roar.
What though the fall renewed the wounds and tore
His flesh, and jarred His head so crudely crowned!

They come to the Praetorium, vacant now, and quiet since the shouting Jews had left, since the faithless inhabitants had departed to their homes, subdued and frightened at the strange darkness. There is the spot where He had accepted the cross:

For this is all the kingly city gives —
A cursed fig-tree, and a tree of blood:
Denuded, ribald, it no longer lives,
Bereft of branches, shorn of bark and bud.

Above — Mary looks up that flight of marble steps — above on the platform was the place where Pilate had condemned the Sun of Justice to death — coward Pilate, wavering between truth and falsehood, between politics and justice, between conscience and ambition; Pilate, superficial and pompous, crying out: "I am guiltless of the blood of this just man!" And that bit of temporizing had drawn from the Jews the fearful curse: "His blood be upon us and upon our children!"

"Sub Pontio Pilato," down the years
Before a man may truly live, reborn
Of water and the Holy Ghost, he hears,
Caught in the Creed, those words of pitying scorn
For him whose heart was meager, not malign,
Who used ironic water for a sign.

Mary sobs a prayer for Pilate who after all was one of the sons given her from the cross. She breathes a pitying prayer for Pilate's wife, who had pleaded with her husband to have nothing to do with the Satin-inspired business of condemning a God to death.

Then, still sobbing, this Mother of Divine Compassion utters a prayer for the Jews, her own kinsfolk, that what they had screamed as a curse might turn into a blessing for them, and for all the world: His Sacred Blood be upon them, and upon their children, as a laver of regeneration, to bring them finally back to true spiritual kinship with Him in His kingdom — which is not of this world.

4. IF YOU HAD GONE TO MARY

Somewhere, Judas, back in the beginning of your apostleship, there must have crept into your mind a doubt of the Master, a criticism of His policies and methods. That was the time to go to Mary. You could have told her all: you were puzzled, you did not understand His way of proceeding, you thought He was making a mistake.

But you were ashamed of your disloyalty then; you hid the thought. Did you really think you were hiding it from Jesus? And it might have been that Mary, too, knew and was watching with anxious heart, waiting for a chance to warn you, advise you. Perhaps you felt that had you told the Mother, she would have counseled you to leave His company, and you were not ready to take so decisive an action — yet.

How did you come to join His company in the first place? We cannot imagine that you would cry out: "Lord, depart from me, for I am a sinful man," as did St. Peter. We have no record that you hesitated, like Nathaniel, asking if anything good could come from Nazareth. Yet it is not likely that you obeyed a look, a brief command "Follow Me" as in the case of other Apostles. Certain it is that He chose you — He said so; and surely, you must have started your apostleship with the same enthusiasm, trust, and high hopes as the other eleven experienced.

Then came a time when it was all so boring, so disappointing — everything was going wrong; nobody appreciated your obvious capabilities. The heaviest burdens were put on you, yes, and you performed your tasks cleverly. But for you, the Apostles might have gone hungry many a time; yet no one praised your economic system. Actually, one would think Matthew would have been chosen as Business Manager; but evidently you, of all those that followed Him, were the only one that sensed the need of saving, the wisdom of storing up some of the treasures that the grateful people were showering upon the Master and His followers.

During that last year, especially, you had felt that you were in an intellectual desert. If Jesus were God,

He was too occupied with the things of the spirit to be aware of the really pressing urgency of the political situation. If He were only man, He was still an impractical visionary, prattling of falling sparrows, the numbered hairs of one's head, and the glory of field lilies — all very poetic, but it wasn't getting them anywhere.

Why didn't you go to Mary then, Judas? Why didn't you tell her how imprudently and prodigally her Son was acting? But no. If no one praised you, at least you would not risk incurring blame; not, that is, until the time Mary of Bethany poured the precious ointment on His feet. Then it was that your irritation burst its bounds and seethed over into the criticism: "This ointment might have been sold . . ." Then, feeling the disapproval around you, you added quickly: "and given to the poor."

The Master knew. He turned to you gently: "The poor you have always with you. What she has done, she has done for My burial." That was a warning. Did the others notice? It is possible that you were the only one that read through His veiled reference to His death. You could have gone to Mary then, Judas. You could have asked of her an explanation of His words; you could have told her your fears that His kingdom would not after all be established on earth.

Your insecurity was mounting. You were so lonely; and all about you, your companions had continued their absorption in the Master and His teaching. John, there, was hanging on His every word. But you had heard it all before — it all seemed to follow the same pattern — and it all led nowhere and to nothing. Hence, since these amazing three years were about to culminate in failure and death, why shouldn't you get your just reward before it was too late? Oh Judas, if only you had gone to Mary with these thoughts. But you went to the High Priest.

Was it too late then? With the thirty pieces of silver added to the funds at your cincture, with your promise to deliver Him at the earliest opportunity, with spies dogging your footsteps lest the traitor should prove doubly traitorous — was it too late? No. Mary would have shown you a way out.

So you worked out your plan. You had need of all your subtlety and cleverness — there were so many to be deceived, so much of your procedure had to be hidden. Again and again you felt the Master had discovered your perfidy. Toward the end, you feared He might even devise some way of keeping you in the supper room and forcing you to fail the appointment you had with the High Priest. But no — He even made it easier for you to get out. After His breath-taking announcement of the betrayal, He turned to you directly, reaching to you the bread, and saying:

"What thou dost, do quickly."

Some of the Apostles even looked at you with respect: here at the most solemn celebration of the Paschal feast, the Master was sending you out on an errand.

Thus you left the brightly lighted chamber. Outside — it was dark. Someone was helping you now, Judas. Someone was fearing that plans like these should not be trusted to a weak and vacillating human being. So Satan entered into you. It was Satan who was guiding your course of action. Was it too late, then, to go to Mary? No. Her heel would have been set upon the slimy Arch Traitor, she could have freed you from those throttling coils. You could have doubled back upon

your course, sought for Mary (you may be sure she was
not far from that Supper Chamber) called upon her
for help, flung the thirty pieces of silver at *her* feet, and
flung yourself at the feet of the Master. Perhaps Satan
feared you would do just that; he snarled your thoughts
into a confused urge to hasten and complete your work.

The High Priest had his servants and soldiers waiting for you. You were put in command of them. Here
was a momentary surge of joy; they praised your
tactics, they looked to you for guidance. Here at last
your native gift for organization was recognized. You
gave directions, you emphasized the necessity for quiet,
for waiting until just the exact moment.

The Three Hours Agony was agony for you in a different sense. Suppose something should go wrong at
the last moment? Suppose the Master should escape,
should disappear, leaving you to play the fool, to confess your failure, to relinquish the thirty pieces of silver
to the High Priest and his minions?

But so far, things were going well. Silently, by
circuitous route, you were leading the crowd out from
the city gates, over the brook, up the hill. From tree to
tree they slipped, tracking their prey. A difficulty
arose: it was dark — the Master would be surrounded
by His apostles. How should they know which one to
capture? How could they prevent some one of the
devoted followers, John for example, from posing as
the Master and being captured in His stead? You had
a solution for their doubts:

"Whomsoever I shall kiss — that is He . . ." and you
added, quite unnecessarily, but perhaps to impress
them with the power of their prisoner: "Hold Him
fast."

So the kiss was given — your bargain was sealed.

Was it too late then, to go to Mary? No — even then, she would have shown the way out; she would have devised a plan for you. When despair settled upon your soul, when you realized that your treachery had been successful indeed, when you saw He was not going to elude His captors; when in a blinding but too-late light you realized that He was God — yet Man, innocent, yet condemned; and that He was delivered through your betrayal: after all that, was it too late to go to Mary? No. She would have been then, as she has been ever since: the Refuge of sinners, the Comforter of the afflicted, the Lady of Good Counsel to those in torturing doubt.

But you went to the High Priest. You made to the priests the confession you should have made to Jesus, or to His Mother. When Peter denied his Lord, he did not seek a halter to choke out the life that was heavy with sin. Very likely *he* went to Mary, the Queen of the Apostles, who became for him a tower of strength and a gate to the heaven that awaited him after his repentance.

But you found a halter, and a dark, lonely tree, with its stark limb outlined against a lurid sky. And when your Master hung upon the Tree of Salvation, you were breathing out your twisted, gasping life on a tree of damnation — your own choice. Even then, with the last gasp, the last thought, you might have turned interiorly to the Hope of the Dying. But the despairing end came. Yes. It was too late, then, Judas, to go to Mary.

❊   ❊   ❊

When the death on the Cross had freed the world; when the darkness that had covered the earth had begun to disappear; when Mary and John, Nicodemus

and Joseph had performed the last sad rites for Jesus'
mangled Body, had with reverence and love washed
away the blood, the spittle and defilement; had a-
nointed the fever-swollen wounds, wrapped the sacred
limbs, in sweet, clean linen, and laid Him in the new-
hewn tomb, nobody performed a similar rite for you,
Judas. Your body had not then been discovered, creak-
ing dismally against that halter as the wind swung it
to and fro. When it was found, it was cut down,
wrapped hastily, deposited with crude dispatch in the
field that was the ultimate result of your bargaining.

But it may have been, as John led Mary back from
Calvary, that a crouching figure obstructed their way,
that despairing sobs came to their ears. In spite of
John's protests, Mary the Mother of sorrow, would
have gone to raise and comfort the poor creature. John,
wonderingly, might have said:

"Mary, how could any sorrow be like to your sorrow?
How can you spare time and sympathy apart from your
own grief?" and Mary would have answered:

"Oh, my son, did you not know? That was the
mother of Judas."

You did not go to Mary, Judas — but it would have
been so like Mary to go to your mother.

5. JOY OF ISRAEL

(In thanks for a statue — hand-carved — from Rome
— of a lovely Lady, grief sculpted — in Jerusalem)

Our Lady of Sorrows! your arm
cradles not a child
but a sword.
O Mother mild,
Mother of the Lord,

you would shield from harm
the wayward ones who forged the sword
to pierce your heart:
You cradle-sheathe it lest it dart
against your wayward ones
for whom He died.
O daughter, mother, bride
of God, you brought *Him* forth from joy to pain
that we be brought from sin-linked chain
to joy and final cease
of pain, sweet Queen of Peace.

6. FROM FRIDAY TO SUNDAY

(I St. Peter 3:19)

"Behold the Lamb of God! Behold Him who has taken away the sins of the world!"

St. John's clarion voice rang through the dim, gray vaults of Limbo. Then, on his knees before his Saviour-Cousin, he asked: "How is Mary, Lord? How is my Lady of the Magnificat, whom I greeted even in my mother's womb?"

"She is in the care of my beloved disciple," answered Jesus, "she will be comforted and strengthened when he exercises the priestly faculties which I gave him last night."

St. Joseph started up from his long quiescence to greet his Foster-Son, and the question on his lips was:

"My wife? Where is she? We have sought You sorrowing, but what of her whom You left sorrowing on earth?"

"She must remain a little longer, Joseph. She is needed to nurse My mystical Body, which will continue the work I have begun."

Simeon came through the darkened aisles, his eyes blinking at the sudden light, his arms outstretched:

"Now wilt Thou dismiss Thy servant, according to Thy word, in peace," he greeted. "And, Lord God, how is the little maid whose heart the sword has pierced?"

"She is pondering your prophecy, she is realizing its fulfillment, Simeon, and she is holding all these things in her heart."

And then our Lord went on, walking between the kneeling figures, who were paying Him deepest reverence: Anna spoke to him of all that looked for the redemption of Israel; often had they heard her tell of His presentation in the Temple. They never tired of hearing her describe the gentle, sweet woman who brought him there, offering in sacrifice two young pigeons.

Elizabeth reached out longing hands to Him, crying: "Whence is this to me, that my Lord should come at last? And where is she, Jesus, whose spirit rejoiced in God her Saviour?"

"She is sorrowing now," answered Jesus, "but yet a little while and her joy will return."

Zachary greeted Him with the canticle of prophecy that now had new meaning:

"Blessed be the Lord God of Israel, because He hath visited and wrought redemption to his people . . . in holiness and justice before Him, all our days. And thou, Child," he turned to his son who was accompanying Our Lord, "thou hast indeed gone before Him to prepare the way. But now He Himself has given knowledge of salvation to His people, unto the remission of their sins. And He has come to enlighten them that sit in this darkness and in this shadow of death — now will He direct our feet in the way of peace."

So back through the centuries of souls went the Crucified:

Isaias repeated exultantly his prophecy: "Verily thou art a hidden God, the God of Israel, the Saviour . . . the forgers of errors are gone together in confusion . . . they esteemed Him a worm and no man, but Thou, Lord shalt go forth as a mighty man, a man of war, and Thou shalt prevail over thine enemies. Now wilt thou bring forth the prisoner out of prison, and them that sit in darkness out of the prison house. But — can a woman forget her infant, so as not to have pity on the son of her womb? And neither can we forget, Lord God, the love and pity of her who bore thee. Her name is as oil poured out!"

Our Lord smiled His appreciation: "And all generations shall indeed call her blessed, Isaias. She is pondering the old prophecies in faith and peace. Her time will come."

David looked at Him and chanted his most joyful praise:

"Shout with joy to God, all the earth, and sing ye a psalm to his name . . . blessed be God, who hath not turned away my prayer, nor his mercy from me."

Ruth knelt at His feet, lovingly, and repeated to Him her prayer of fidelity: "Entreat me not to leave Thee, nor return from following after Thee . . . for whither Thou goest, I will go."

Esther cried out to Him: "I see thee, my Lord, as One sent from God, and my heart is troubled for fear of Thy Majesty! Blessed be the womb that bore Thee!"

Judith, too, regal in her graciousness, though her beauty was dimmed in the gray halls of Limbo, swept forward to do Him honor and sang her canticle: "Sing ye to the Lord with cymbals, tune unto Him a new

psalm, for Thou hast put an end to wars, O Lord . . .
let us sing a hymn to the Lord, let us sing a new hymn
to our God." Then she applied to Mary the blessing
which Ozias the prince of the people had proclaimed
upon her in her victory over the general Holofernes:

"And blessed is she who bore Thee, Lord most high
God, above all the women upon the earth."

Finally, in His progress, the Crucified One came to
Eve, who looked eagerly into the shining Face:

"My Lord and my God!" she worshiped Him, and
then came the breathless query:

"And Mary? Did her heel crush the serpent's head?"

Jesus answered: "Ah, Mother of all the living, and
My mother Eve, the long wait is over. Yet a little, and
you shall come with Me to Paradise. All of you shall
enter in with Me, and take possession of the Kingdom
I have won for you."

❁　　　❁　　　❁

Jesus came to Mary Easter morning — very early, before the sun arose: "Oh, Queen of Heaven, rejoice!"
He cried, "I have been to Limbo, and all our beloved
friends, kindred, and forerunners were asking for you.
Their sorrowful waiting is over, and now they are
waiting joyously to welcome you into the Kingdom
prepared for you and for them. But, Mother, I need
you to nurse the Infant Church; I need you to guide
My Apostles, and tend the first fruits of My Passion.
Mother, will you wait yet a little while?"

And Mary bowed her head: "Behold the handmaid
of the Lord."

VIII

APRIL

Speaking liturgically, we consider April two seasons. According to the year, it might begin with the most sorrowful "Great Week," the Week of the Passion. But it is likely that the greater part of the month would be the celebration of your Son's Resurrection. So — especially during Holy Week, we consider the mystery of evil as shown in the example of Judas. For that, I have let my imagination and devotion play around in the sketch: "If you had gone to Mary." O Mary, perhaps you gave him so many opportunities — if only — even after he had flung those coins down — if only . . . but these "if only's" are mere speculation. It all comes back to the mystery of the God-given freedom of will. In all Jesus' public life, He never commanded that. He always asked (as prelude to a great grace) "Wilt thou?" He never asked leprosy or blindness or devil possession or diseases of various kinds if *they* wanted to leave their victims in peace. He commanded them. He commanded the winds and the waves, He commanded the devils; but in the case of the human will, He said humbly: "Wilt thou?" So Judas willed evil. But Peter! Surely brave, candid Peter must have gone to you after his three-fold denial. How otherwise could he have endured himself and his cowardice?

Then, too, since Holy Week includes a visit to Limbo (St. Peter says "coming, He preached to those that were in prison"), here is this other fancy: that during our Lord's progress to the "souls in prison" from the most recently dead back through the centuries to Eve, each and all must have asked you; you the long-promised one, whose heel had crushed the serpent's head, whose heart the sword of sorrow pierced.

On the first of April, my Mother, our Sr. Esther celebrates her feast: whether her patron is some obscure little "beata" that isn't even mentioned in the records, or whether the name is a form of the word "east" — the Orient, therefore *rising*, hence the feast is in celebration of the Resurrection; or whether her patron is the Esther of the Old Testament and therefore the date is arbitrarily chosen, I have not been able to ascertain.

But certainly sweet Mother, as Esther, niece of Mordecai, is considered a prototype of you, she is worthy of veneration. Like yourself, she was an exile in this vale of tears, and the Jewish people of her time dwelt in captivity, just as they in your time had been subjugated to the Romans. Like yourself being preferred over Eve, the mother of all the living who was disobedient to the command of God, so Esther was preferred over Vashti, who refused to come at the king's command. Like yourself, she was chosen "from among thousands," for one who should please the eyes of the king. Like you, she was exceedingly fair and beautiful, and she found favor and was pleasing to the king. Also like you, she risked death and disgrace to stand before the king and plead for her people.

But O my Mother, Mother of Mercy, the resemblance ends there. For Esther, in her interview with the king, is represented as "fainting for very delicacy,"

so that she was upheld by her maids, while you, my
Mother, you *stood* beneath the cross. You were different in another way: for Esther, having obtained the
reversal of the king's decree for the slaughter of the
Jews, was triumphantly and vengefully insistent that
the decree should be turned against those who plotted
against her people. She was not satisfied until Aman
and his ten sons were hanged upon gibbets. The
further account of the slaughter: five hundred men in
the city of Susan should have been enough according
to the king's opinion (and he a pagan!) but at Esther's
request the killing continued until it amounted to
seventy-five thousand, not only in Susan, but throughout the provinces under the king's jurisdiction. All
this savagery is hard to credit, Mother. For even in
the Old Testament the Father, the Creator, is represented as a Father of Mercy and Compassion.

When your Son, Mary, spoke so beautifully of His
Father and of His characteristics, Philip was moved
to exclaim: "Lord, show us the Father and it is enough
for us." But Jesus answered that He and His Father
are one. Even without the knowledge of these characteristics of compassion and mercy, the disciples
might have formed a picture of their merciful, loving
God from any mention of God as *Father* (since it
remained for Jesus to come and tell about the Holy
Trinity), but a glance at a Scriptural Concordance
would reveal countless expressions like: "His mercies
are many; the multitude of thy tender mercies; thy
mercies are from the beginning; Lord God, merciful,
gracious, and patient; the Lord thy God is a merciful
God; the mercy which He swore to thy fathers; the
ways of the Lord are mercy and truth; mercy belongeth

to thee, O Lord; My mercy I will not take away."
Likewise there are comparable references to such words
as compassion, kindness, understanding, forgiveness.
So, vengeful, unyielding Esther is not a counterpart of
you, my Mother of Mercy!

April twenty-sixth, Mary, is the feast suggested by
one of your miraculous pictures: that of Our Lady of
Good Counsel. This is really miraculous in that it is
represented on a thin, seemingly fragile scale of wall
plaster suspended in the air without visible support.
On St. Mark's day, in the midst of a fiesta, it came
shrouded in a fleecy cloud that descended and fixed
itself within the sight of the people, facing the walls
of a pious widow's unfinished church — a church in the
little town of Genazzano, about twenty-five miles
southeast of Rome. It was called Petruccia's folly,
because, although she claimed she was commanded to
build a church, she had not been able to finish it. In
the face of opposition and ridicule, she prophesied
that the church would be finished before her death,
and that a great lady would come to take possession
of it. Oh Mary, Mary, you *do* have a way of getting
your wishes fulfilled!

When all the fiesta crowd had riveted their attention
on this cloud clinging to the wall like a new swarm
of bees, the cloud parted, showing in its midst a lovely
picture of Madonna and Child. At the same time, all
the bells in the city began to ring without any human
hands on the ropes.

This picture, Mary, shows you turning to your Child,
who has caught hold of your dress at the chest line,
His other hand around your neck. He seems to be
whispering to you. It is called Our Lady of Good

Counsel, not because He seems to be giving you good counsel to pass on to others, but because that was already the name of Petruccia's church. The picture has been preserved for us, Mary, even though during the World War a bomb came crashing through the roof of the basilica (oh yes, of course, it was finished and finished according to the widow's prophecy, and stood intact for nearly five hundred years). The bomb destroyed the high altar, reduced to rubble all the beautiful things in the sanctuary; yet your picture only a few yards away and so brittle in its eggshell thickness was preserved intact, in fact unshaken.

There is a little hymn, sweet Mother, which has been a consolation to many a child, many a person seeking to know her vocation, and to many a child-like heart of maturer years:

"O Virgin Mother, Lady of Good Counsel,
Sweetest picture artist ever drew,
In all doubts, I fly to thee for guidance —
Mother tell me, what am I to do."

How I loved it in the early days, when I used to say: "I have a vocation that refuses to vocate!"

The Second Sunday after Easter, Mother, is known as Good Shepherd Sunday. A companion to this is your feast (proper only in some dioceses) under the title "Mother of the Divine Shepherd." It is set for September third, but it parallels your Son's April feast, in that just as the Sunday of the Good Shepherd comes after all His suffering and triumph, and before the re-starting of the year's cycle of feasts for Him, so your feast comes after your glorious Assumption and before the re-commencement of your life's cycle of feasts.

The first prayer of the Collect for this Mother-of-Divine Shepherd feast of yours, Mother, is consoling: "O Lord Jesus Christ, good Shepherd who hast given Thy life for Thy sheep, and while hanging on the cross didst commend Thy people, the sheep of Thy pasture, to Thy Virgin Mother, grant that through her intercession we, having followed Thee as our Pastor on earth, may be led to the pastures of everlasting life."

My Mother, good Shepherdess of the sheep, even of those that are lost and fumbling in darkness and thorns and famine, pray for us!

Here, harking back to the Old Testament picture of God the Father, and showing the appropriateness of the Shepherd symbol, we have the description that Ezechiel writes:

"Thus saith the Lord God: Behold, I myself will come upon my shepherds, and I will require my flock at their hand . . . Behold, I myself will seek My sheep and will visit them . . . and will deliver them out of all the places where they have been scattered in the cloudy and dark day . . . and I will feed them in the mountains, by the rivers, and in all the habitations of the land. I will feed them in the most fruitful pastures, and their pastures shall be in the high mountains; there shall they rest on the green grass, and be fed in fat pastures upon the mountains of Israel. I will seek that which was lost; and that which was driven away, I will bring back again; and I will bind up that which was broken, and I will strengthen that which was weak, and that which was fat and strong I will preserve."

My Mother, good Shepherdess, call that passage to the attention of our God, the Father of Mercy, won't you, and intercede for those who are scattered in the cloudy and dark day of false philosophy, misleading **ideologies, deceit, and tyranny?** Sheep aren't noted for their intelligence, my Mother — in fact, they are amazingly stupid — O Mother, take care of them and bring them back to your Son's fold!

IX

1. MAY

The beginning of this month, Mary, is the beginning of "May Devotions" the origin of which I tried to trace for you in the article "Fairest of Seasons."

The beginning of your month is a joyous day for us; but it is also the "May Day" for the Soviets, and yearly they are celebrating with grim and triumphant recognition of their seeming success. Oh, Mother Mary, how CAN you let this go on? In 1917 you came to the children at Fatima and said in effect: "Pray for Russia; unless prayer and penance are offered, the world will be rent with an even more horrible War than that which is going to end soon." Yet — since then, the Communists have been gaining ground.

Evidently the people (meaning me among others) did not pray enough, did not do enough penance; for, not twenty years later, the world was certainly shredded with an incredibly more terrible and unjust war! And in every conflict, no matter who "won," the Communists were the substantial gainers. We say prayers after Low Mass for the conversion of Russia. Won't you answer them? Perhaps we do not pray hard enough, with sufficient attention, with sufficient awareness.

It is such a mystery! In all newspapers, magazines, books, the evils of Communism are discussed, proved, exemplified: the treachery of the Russians in Korea, China, and the European countries, their aggressions

against the United States (and our meekness and
"protests" produce still bolder and more frightening
incidents), the penetration of the Communistic ideol-
ogy into the very citadel of the Government – traitors
in high places. We read all this, we the common people, and I among others exclaim: "How is it that the
leaders of our country, those in power and able to *do*
something, don't know this and take proper action!"

Then I feel, sweet Mother, that you should appear
to our President, Ambassadors, and to the others of
great minds and will – the leaders of the world, to tell
them what to do. But these are very foolish thoughts
of mine, because I know from the history of the world
and from my own life-long experience (and that of
others) that you just don't do things that way. And
for answer (if you answered), you would call attention
to our Lord's parable of Dives and Lazarus: "Even if
one rose from the dead . . ."

You have your own ways of getting your will done
and of getting souls to spread the Kingdom of your
Son. I shall have to trust and submit and keep on
praying. There is indeed cause for serious concern in
the success of the Soviets in spreading their doctrine,
in planting turmoil within so that Chinese are fighting
Chinese; Koreans, Koreans; in fact the natives of every
country tainted with their vicious, slimy methods have
resorted to civil war – the very thing Soviets wanted
in order to have an excuse to step in and bring
"freedom" – their kind of freedom. Not only has there
been that kind of success, but there have been more
insidious inroads in our country: Great men with
seemingly honest and trustworthy characters have de-
fected to the cause of Communism. There is the
terrifying view of the map of Soviet domination: most

of Europe and Asia, dangerously near to the United States; there is the careless indifference of those who do not embrace Soviet Doctrine themselves, but do the devil's work in their defeatist attitude: "I'm not in sympathy with the Soviets, but I am anti-anti-Communist. Let them alone; let's not have witch-burning; it's only politics; and besides, it can't happen here."

But in all this there has been one thought, my Mother, to which I have clung for encouragement and confidence: We must still believe it is your Son's world and He died to redeem it. His will *will be done* — otherwise we could not believe and teach that He is the Supreme Power. There have been other instances in history where what seemed to be the most irrevocable tragedy has been turned into blessing:

I look back over the captivity of the Jews — the Babylonian Captivity especially. Many at that time must have wondered HOW their very own God could let it happen (even though they knew that then, as now, the people had their own unfaithfulness to blame). It must have seemed at the time that it was the very worst thing that could happen; but God used their downfall to spread the knowledge of His oneness and beauty and truth to the pagans and the earnest seekers, so that the Jews spiritually conquered their conquerors and were themselves purified in their misfortunes, turning to God in humble supplication and recognition of the justice of their punishment.

It must have seemed to the many nations, victims of Rome, that their overthrow and the conquest of most of the known world by Rome was irremediable tragedy — but it was through this conquest that Christianity reached to far places. Even the very material and practical devices of the Romans — good roads, for example, were instrumental in this. Certainly the avowed purpose of the Roman masters was not to make opportunity for the spread of Christianity — but I like to think that many a slave stonebreaker, secretly a Christian, toiling in the hot, back-breaking labor of road building, must have found consolation in the thought that he was another John the Baptist, preparing the way, making the rough paths straight, filling up the valleys and ravines, that the disciples of Christ might have access to further fields of zeal.

So now; it is different, yes, because so far as we know in the early days, even pagan ideals *were* ideals; they knew the difference between truth and lies, and they embraced truth, honesty, and reliability as far as they knew. In early times, men *did* have a standard of right and wrong (at least so we might interpret history). But now the devil seems to have succeeded in twisting standards in such a way that what was truth today is lies tomorrow; that the very vices of complicity, treachery, and lying become — not virtues (that's an old-fashioned word), but clever devices for the cause of Communism. It is horribly true that brain-washing of Soviet victims has succeeded in making even the unwilling and right-intentioned captives confuse the wrong with the right.

There are no standards for the Soviets; they expect their enemies to practice truth and decency; for them, there is only expediency. Yes — there seems to be mass perversion, but I know well it can be overcome by God's methods, individual by individual, just as each grain of wheat comes to maturity, each flower to the one development, each soul to its own fulfillment.

Sweet Mother, in my imagination (that plaything of the mind!) I take the place of — say an airman shot down and wounded, captured by the Chinese Reds, tended more or less adequately by Chinese doctors, but his physical treatment interspersed by doses of Communistic doctrine. Why couldn't the airman explain to the Chinese doctors how efficient and germ-proof and merciful are our American hospital standards and methods? Why shouldn't the airman point to his very body — with its good teeth, muscular coordination, as proof that good food, balanced activity, freedom of action, education, and worship had produced the kind of being that would not be susceptible to propaganda, however subtle? And if his hearers further doubt, they could be invited to come and see! And suppose the question is brought up about our treatment of Negroes and Indians, could not the reply be: "So far as we have failed there, it is because we have not put in practice the ideals of toleration and mercy on which democracy was founded; just as when a Christian is blamed for a life of vice: he's just not living up to Christian standards."

Yes — but my mind goes back to the traitors in our own country: good food, balanced activity, security, comfort, and all the rest in which we exult and for which we are truly grateful, have not prevented them — many of our most brilliant minds — from embracing pagan doctrines, false philosophy, treacherous ideals. In fact, the very reason that traitors have penetrated with subversive activities is that our freedom of speech and press allow it — it all goes back to that problem of free will again.

But then, Mother, that playful imagination of mine goes on to place me myself, a religious, in the kind of situation that has been frequently described in regard to missionaries in Red China. This of course might be dangerous presumption if I take it seriously — and I could only dismiss the thought by assuring God that I would rely on His Divine Providence. On the other hand — so much of the questioning of the missionaries seems so childish and unreasonable that I propose that a Religious should take such an attitude as she would observe toward a fractious pupil — show him how far below human standards he is acting, how utterly absurd are the claims that she is a spy, or an enemy, or a danger to the men, women, and children for whose bodies and souls she has previously shown such solicitude.

You manage it all, Mother — and oh! with all the love and appreciation of my heart I pray you to obtain special graces for those missionaries who are still behind the curtain: whether iron, bamboo, or ideological. Obtain for them light, O Lady of light! Obtain for them guidance, O Lady of Good Counsel!

For May thirteenth, we have your feast of Fatima. Between Fatima and Lourdes we have the whole gamut of your honors: at Lourdes you manifested to Bernadette the privilege of your Immaculate Conception, and at Fatima we have the last — or rather the latest of your attributes, Mary — Mediatress of Graces. The devout mind loves to dwell on those contrasts, Mother: we love to ferret out the oldest and the newest, the first and the last, the greatest and smallest, the most renowned — and the most obscure.

The oldest of your shrines is one that was (so tradition says) erected even before the coming of Christianity. It is in that favorite jeweled Cathedral of yours, Chartres. Here you have imitated so many of your favorite Frenchmen by going "underground."

We are told that Chartres, before the time of Julius Caesar, was an important seat of worship where the Druids erected an altar to the *Virgo Paritura*. Here was set up a statue of you holding your Baby, who in turn holds a globe in His left hand. This statue — oh, shame! — was destroyed by the French Revolutionists, but reconstructed afterwards according to the description still kept on record. While I am on the subject of Chartres, Mother, I recall that this privileged cathedral has also a relic of your veil. Oh Mary! There are so few relics of yours; in fact, this is the only authentic one that I know of. Shrines yes — great and small, old and new — but no relics.

The newest? The newest and smallest and most obscure might be the one lately erected in the classroom of some Catholic school, all bedecked with blue and white tissue paper. Or, perhaps, even newer and smaller and more obscure, erected in the bedroom of a small child who brings to you her treasures, her love of your beauty, her longing to venerate you fittingly. It was because of such a shrine, my Mother, that I wrote for you the story of "Our Lady's Revenge." It is true in part — and the part that is merely fiction is the kind of thing you'd do anyway.

May seventeenth is the feast of a devoted son of yours, St. Paschal Baylon, a shepherd, a Franciscan. He is renowned for his devotion to the Blessed Sacrament, but also for his zeal in your interest, Mary. He learned to read with the sole motive of being able to say your Little Office. That recalls your command to Lucia of Fatima, Mary. You told her among other things to learn to read. Our Lady of Readers (slow, avid, retarded, or whatever) pray for your clients.

Our Lady, Help of Christians, we celebrate your feast May twenty-fourth. It is a tribute of gratitude to you instituted by Pius VII on his return to Rome, after his three-year imprisonment by Napoleon. Mother mine! Why can't tyrants learn that they CANNOT fight against your Son and your Son's Vicar without insuring their own downfall! We sometimes salute you this day as our Lady of Victory, sweet Mother, but your real feast under this title comes October seventh. It was established under this title to celebrate the Naval Victory near Lepanto — and surely this is another basis for confidence in you as mediatress: for centuries the Spaniards had fought seemingly a losing battle against the Moors. The Spaniards had formed what seemed the only bulwark (and a frail one at that!) to prevent the Moors from over-running all Europe. But with the help of the valiant Austrians, victory for you and for your Son's cause came at last. Doesn't that suggest something for you to do in regard to the Soviets, Mother?

There is another shrine for you called "Our Lady of Victories." This is in Paris, and has special claim to our interest because it was there that the Little Flower was taken by her devoted Papa to see the sights. For her, there was only one sight: your statue, Our Lady of Victories. It was at this shrine that you told her distinctly that it was you who had cured her earlier, and it was here she entreated you to enfold her forever in the protection of your cloak.

For the thirty-first, what a riotous wealth of feasts we have, Mother! It is as though you want the month to go out in a glory, a special preparation for your Son's month of the Sacred Heart. Our Lady of the Sacred

Heart, Our Lady Mediatress of all graces, Our Lady Mother of Beautiful Love, Our Lady Queen of All Saints. And then this last one which your devoted son Pius XII gave to all the world: a feast under your title: "Queenship of Mary."

Under two of these titles: that of Queen of All Saints and that of Mother of Beautiful Love, we have for the Epistle of the proper Mass that wonderfully eloquent description from Wisdom:

"I have stretched out my branches as the turpentine tree, my branches are of honor and grace. As the vine, I have brought forth a pleasant odor; and my flowers are the fruit of honey and riches. I am the mother of fair love, and of fear, and of knowledge, and of holy hope. In me is all the grace of the way and the truth; in me is all hope of life and of virtue. Come over to me, all you that desire me, and be filled with my fruits. For my spirit is sweet above honey, and my inheritance above honey and the honeycomb. My memory is unto everlasting generations. They that eat me shall yet hunger, and they that drink me shall yet thirst. He that hearkeneth to me shall not be confounded; and they that work by me shall not sin. They that explain me shall have life everlasting."

O Mary, I could not resist quoting all of this exquisitely beautiful passage, for it seems the answer to all my complaints about Sovietism and the power of evil. What else but these consoling words have you been saying to your children, whether in actual apparition or in secret inspiration all these years?

And in all these pages, I've been trying to "work by you" and "explain" you, Mary, so don't forget about the life everlasting for me.

2. THE FAIREST OF SEASONS

Rome — springtime — 1858. It is three months after a lovely Lady who proclaimed herself the Immaculate Conception had appeared to Bernadette in the cave of Massabielle at Lourdes, commanded a church to be built, and asked for processions. But here in Rome on this gentle May day there is no apparition, no revelation, no command:

A little boy kneels in the dusty street not far from a small statue of Mary erected as a shrine by the wayside. In his mind is re-echoing some praise of the sweet Lady — praises he had heard in church he says:

"Tower of Ivory, House of Gold, Ark of the Covenant . . ."

Another child passes, looks at him curiously, then joins him and makes the responses:

> "Gate of Heaven
> > pray for us
> Morning Star
> > pray for us."

It is evening, the twilight is settling down like a cloak. A few more children join the first two. Not all can remember the Litany, but they utter whatever phrases they can think of. Then through the quiet air comes a summons; mothers are calling their children home:

"Antonio! Maria! Giuseppe! Giovanni!" and the children scatter.

The next evening they are there again, and each time the crowd increases. They are joined by some

women, curious to see what is going on, and perhaps
somewhat relieved that their little ones are so harm-
lessly occupied.

A priest from a nearby church comes up to them.
He is attracted by the rhythmic chanting of the Litany
and the hymn they have now added. He listens a
while, and then says:

"Come into the church, children — and you older
ones. We will light candles at Mary's altar, and then
we will all say the Litany together, and sing a hymn
to her. After that, I will give you my blessing."

That is how May Devotions started — and that they
have originated with children is so characteristic of
things pertaining to Mary.

Of course, the consecration of the Month of May to
Mary was not new. In ancient Rome, the pagan
Romans had consecrated May to the *Bona Dea* — the
goddess of fertility in nature, the patroness of fruitful-
ness and chastity in women. When Rome became
the center and stronghold of Christianity, what more
natural than that May should become Mary's month?

Then too, there was a somewhat older and more
formal attempt to initiate special devotions to Mary in
May:

Somewhere around 1790, Father Latona, head of the
Roman College of the Society of Jesus, became sadly
aware that something must be done about the increasing faithlessness and immorality among students.
To counteract these evil forces, he made a vow to de-
vote the month of May to Mary, and to say some
special prayers in her honor. This custom spread to
other houses of the Society of Jesus, so that by the
time our little boy knelt in the dust to chant his frag-

ment of Litany, even the children were accustomed to saluting Mary with extra devotion during the time when the weather was sweetest.

All good things in grace come to us through Mary: it is most fitting that we should associate with her all that is lovely in nature: flowers, gems, snow, the blue sky, the new budding of green things. In the exuberance of our love for her, when all the land is throbbing with the spring, her children sing:

"Bring flowers of the rarest,
Bring flowers of the fairest
   From garden and woodland, and hillside,
      and dale."

There are many hymns to Mary, but those for May are especially associated with the revival of nature after the long winter:

"Green are the leaves and sweet the flowers,
   And rich the hues of May"

is the beginning of one song; and another:

"As the gentle spring uncloses
   and the winter fades away."

or again:

"The sun is shining brightly,
   The trees are clothed in green
The beauteous bloom of flowers
   On every side is seen;

The fields are gold and emerald,
    And all the world is gay!
For 'tis the month of Mary,
    The lovely month of May."

Besides those especially seasonal hymns, Mary is honored during her month by some devotions that can be offered to her at any other time. They are manifold:

Saying the Rosary, the Litany, or the Little Office of the Blessed Virgin, or the Little Office of the Immaculate Conception; forming processions, wearing medals and scapulars, decorating pictures and statues, erecting May Altars; membership in Sodalities formed to honor her, and in religious orders, congregations, or societies dedicated to her and founded under her auspices. A study of the origin and history of these customs and practices would pay rich dividends in the way of increased appreciation of Mary.

There is the Rosary, for example. Our Lady gave this devotion to St. Dominic when he was begging her for a weapon against heresy.

Then there is the Litany of Loreto. This was first definitely approved for liturgical use in 1587, but almost all the titles used therein can be traced to the writings ascribed to the Fathers of the first six centuries, or to references in the Old Testament that can be applied to Mary.

Thirdly: the Little Office of the Blessed Virgin has been used ever since the middle of the eighth century, when the Benedictines of Monte Casino added its recitation to that of the Divine Office. It has the same structure as the Divine Office, namely Seven Hours: Matins and Lauds, Prime, Tierce, Sext, None,

Vespers and Complin. All these are comprised of psalms, versicles, responses, hymns, and lessons. So popular was this Office or Mary's "Book of Hours" as it was called in England, that many of the children of the nobility were taught to read from it, and the laity chanted it after daily Mass. Many printed copies of their books, beautifully illuminated and exquisitely decorated, are still kept as priceless treasures in museums and library collections.

Mary has deigned to reward those who honor her by medals, statues, and scapulars; for through these sacramentals have been wrought miracles of cure and miracles of grace. There is the Miraculous Medal, struck according to Catherine Labouré's description of Mary's apparition and request. There is the Miraculous Picture of Our Lady of Perpetual Help. She gave the scapulars to St. Simon Stock with the promise that the wearer would be released from Purgatory on the Saturday after death. Many statues of her have gained the reputation of being miraculous, the latest instance being the pilgrim statue of Our Lady of Fatima.

And processions! Could any form of devotion be more delightful and satisfying? The earliest procession of any significance in a liturgical way was the transferring of the Ark of the Covenant to the Temple which Solomon had built for it. This was a sort of prophetic event which had its fulfillment in the triumphant procession of that first Palm Sunday, when the Holy Spirit inspired the people of Jerusalem to carry palms, sing hosannas, and accompany our Lord to the Temple only five days before His death. Processions as a function of worship occupy an important place in the Church: there is the procession to and from the Sanctuary in connection with the solemn celebration of

Holy Mass; processions of the Blessed Sacrament at Corpus Christi and Holy Thursday; funeral procession, procession of Religious in communities when postulants are to receive the holy habit or novices are to be professed. Then there are processions for some special intention: in thanksgiving, or to plead for suitable weather, abundant harvests, or to prevent storms, famine, plague, or war. All these follow pretty much the same rite: the participants assemble at a given place and march to a determined point — usually a shrine or a church. The leader carries a cross or crucifix, others carry banners or flowers, all join in the hymns and litanies.

These practices, and any others which the piety of the faithful might dictate, have been used during May devotions, and will continue to be used by all generations who call Mary "blessed" and rejoice

> "That God hath so honored our race
>   As to clothe with our nature
>   Sweet Mary, the Mother of grace."

3. UTTERANCE

> "Make me a poem, my Jesus, my Son,
>   Sing me a song for my Queenship feast!"

> "You are My poem, My peerless one,
>   Theme song for souls, the Greatest, the least:
>
>   Mater serena,
>   Gratia plena,
>
> No cadence or strophe, iambic, dactyllic,
>   Fitly encadres your image idyllic."

"Make *me* a poem, my Mother, my Love,

> O clara maris stella
> Et Lucis Dei cella,

Sing me a song of the joys thereof?"

"My child, we shall both be poems of the Maker,

> I, regina Nitoris,
> Solis et Roris,

You the epode, but valiant partaker,
Though confusion-tossed,
Cacaphony lost,

A fragment, a frail one,
Let your dithyramb be aileron,
And my Immaculate Privilege the swift
winged-horse
As medium and craft to Beauty's Prime Source."

4. OUR LADY'S REVENGE

It is not often given to us to see our prayers rounded
out into a perfect answer; it is like catching a glimpse
of a shining star through a long, dark tunnel, giving
assurance that here is the guide to deliverance, the
solution to our problems. The other day a clipping
from a Catholic newspaper brought to mind a prayer
I had made twenty years before. The clipping read:
"Died, suddenly, at his home, Henry A. Thomsen,
a member of the Third Order of St. Dominic. Mr.
Thomsen is survived by a daughter, Sister Mary of
the Assumption, O.C.D. His son, a Missionary of
Mary, died in the Philippines several years ago."

The incident I recalled was this: some twenty years back, little Mary Thomsen was a child in my fifth grade. During the first days of May, she came to me enthusiastically describing her attempts to erect a May Altar at home.

I gave the child a discarded credence cover for her little bedroom table. Her diminutive statue of Mary she raised slightly above table level by means of two volumes of Temple Classics, the dark blue covers of which were not inappropriate for her color scheme. Around the edge of the table she pinned frilled strips of tissue paper left over from the decorations of the classroom altar. For lack of candles and other ornaments, she propped around the base of the blue-book-throne all her little treasures of holy cards and pious leaflets. Two drinking glasses served as vases for the wild flowers she daily collected from fields near the school.

The children helped prepare a May Altar in the classroom, and as she did her share of decorating, Mary, her fair curls billowing on her shoulders, her blue eyes alight with sweet enthusiasm, would tell me of the details of her little bedroom altar. She urged me to come to see it; but she stressed the fact that I must come early in the afternoon, directly after school was out, because Papa . . . and here she broke off and would say no more. Respecting her embarrassment, I answered unconcernedly:

"I'd have to come immediately after school if I came at all; otherwise, I'd be late for prayers. But I'm afraid your May Altar, Mary, is not sufficient excuse for a Religious to go visiting. We do visit the sick and sorrowful, you know — but not May Altars!"

The next day Mary came to school in evident distress, her cheeks blotched with weeping, her eyes downcast. All day the sight of the child wrenched at my heart strings and roused curious glances from the children. I could not stand it when she seemed on the point of leaving without telling me the cause of her grief, or giving me a chance to comfort her. When I called her out of rank, she stood, a pitiful little figure, her shoulders hunched as though to shield herself from cruelly curious glances.

"Tell me, Mary," I pleaded, after the last child had scraped reluctant feet along the corridor, "tell me if I can help you. I have been praying all day for you, because you seem so sorry about something. But if you can't tell me, I'll be distressed to have you go home as sad as when you came."

Then were the flood gates opened:

"Oh, Sister! H-he broke m-my little statue; he threw the h-holy cards down the t-toilet!"

The horror of the seeming sacrilege brought the sobs in gulping breaths. By patient questioning, I elicited the information. Her father was virulently anti-Catholic. She had been warned by her mother not to display any signs of devotion. He was so antagonistic that she and her brother had always to conceal any evidence of their participation in Catholic affairs. May Processions, First Communions, attendance at Mass had always to be attended to clandestinely, lest they arouse their father's fury and even physical punishment. They were allowed to attend the Catholic school only because the public school was further away and overcrowded. Against her mother's advice she had erected the May Altar, for she thought her own little room would be safe from his bigotry; and besides, would not Our Lady take care of her own honor?

What could I say? I could comfort her only by a caress and such soothing ejaculations as I could make to the child who leaned against my knee and pressed her wet cheek against my guimp. Inwardly I was praying with such fierce sincerity as I was ever likely to muster:

"Oh, sweet Mother, take your own revenge. Sweet Mother, you can handle this. It is the kind of thing you permit to happen so that God's way may be revealed to men."

In the end, I think I convinced her that her father, being influenced by passion and ignorance, was probably not morally responsible, and had not burdened his soul with a sin that would condemn him to hell; that he did not hold the holy cards in any esteem at all, and therefore was not committing the sacrilege she thought him guilty of, but that probably he considered the altar an arrogant display of superstition on her part. I told her this occurrence furnished all the more reason for her to continue her prayers for him and not to despair of his salvation. I reminded her of our Lord's prayer for His executioners. I assured her that the breaking of the statue was not an irreparable catastrophe, and I promised her a smaller one that she could keep under her pillow.

I think — oh! the blessed privilege that was mine! — that before she left I gave her some faint understanding of the possibility of vicarious reparation, and of the blessings which, through her prayers, patience, and expiation, such material desecration (so-called) might bring about.

Before the end of the school year, the family moved away, and in time the incident faded from my mind until the newspaper clipping revived it. Some day when class duties are not pressing, I shall take time to get in touch with Sister Mary of the Assumption and learn the story of her father's conversion. I should like to know how that Hound of God, St. Dominic, had driven Mr. Thomsen to the feet of Mary and helped her take her characteristic revenge.

5. LITTLE OFFICE OF THE IMMACULATE CONCEPTION

(A suggestion for enlivening its recitation)

In a somewhat inquiring-reporter style, I conducted an investigation among adults regarding the Little Office of the Immaculate Conception. Most of those approached had been in parochial grade schools or high schools where the Little Office had been recited weekly or monthly by the Children of Mary or by the Sodality. Upon mention of it, even years after, they could automatically swing into:

> Hail Queen of the Heavens,
> Hail mistress of earth,
> Hail Virgin most pure of immaculate birth.

recited in the identical sing-song rhythm they had heard or used week after week or month after month. With a little prompting at the beginning of each "hour," most of them could go through the whole Office.

To the question: "Did you like it?" I received such categorical answers as: "I hated it," or "I loved it," or "I don't know; it didn't make sense, and it didn't make any impression on me, one way or the other."

One who said: "I hated it," mistaking my amused amazement for shock, explained apologetically:

"Well, I suppose it wasn't presented in the right way. I associated it with having to stop an interesting reading hour ahead of time. There were always some disciplinary problems connected with it. We were hustled and crowded into the pews, rushed through the mechanical recitation, and were always later getting home on sodality days. I never knew the meaning of *sodality* or *office*, and while I was not quite so ignorant as the detective in *Murder in a Nunnery* who spoke of the Convent of the 'innaccurate deception,' still that title of our blessed Mother's meant just as little to me as it probably did to him."

Another opinion given by one who loved it was:

"It made me feel so close to Blessed Mother. I didn't know what I was saying, but I knew it was something connected with her, and it gave me something to grow up to. Gradually, as I came in contact with various words and phrases in other connections, I recognized them, and the hymns in the Little Office came to mean more and more."

A third gave as her reason for appreciation:

"It prepared me for the Divine Office, which I was to say after I entered the convent. And any preparation, no matter how remote or mysterious it seemed at the time, is a sacred memory to me now."

Still a fourth opinion was:

"I didn't know the meaning of any of it, but I was sorry when they did away with the recitation of it. I couldn't feel it was a meeting of the Sodality if we didn't say Our Lady's Office; I'm not of those who consider that *all change is progress*."

It is well recognized that any suggested addition to

an already crowded schedule might be met with raised eyebrows, but the interested instructor who would get her class to write out some of the Office verses from memory might receive light and perhaps amusement at the misconceptions divulged. Such an exercise would show the usefulness, perhaps the necessity, of a few minutes' instruction at the beginning of each recitation. A spirited explanation of one phrase or one stanza each time would reap rich results in increased interest and devotion:

The composition of the Little Office is ascribed to St. Alphonsus Liguori, and, like most of his works, it shows his intimate and comprehensive knowledge of the Bible.

The following Scripture references are proposed as points of instruction and development:

QUEEN OF HEAVEN

Jeremias reproached the Jews of old for worshiping the moon, which they called "the queen of heaven." (Jeremias 7:18 and 44:17) He ridiculed the women for making cakes in her honor and protesting: "We will certainly do every word that shall proceed out of our own mouth, to sacrifice to the queen of heaven and to pour out drink offerings to her." St. John in the Apocalypse (12: 1,2, and 5) recognizes the true Queen of Heaven, in his vision: "And a great sign appeared in heaven a woman clothed with the sun, and the moon under her feet, and on her head a crown of twelve stars. And being with child, she cried, travailing in birth; and was in pain to be delivered . . . and she brought forth a man child, who was to rule all nations . . . and her son was taken up to God and to his throne."

VIRGIN MOST PURE OF IMMACULATE BIRTH

Isaias, provoked with the hard-hearted people of his time, who would not turn their thoughts to God and put their trust in Him, cried out: "Therefore the Lord himself shall give you a sign. Behold a virgin shall conceive and bear a son; and his name shall be called Emmanuel." (Isaias 7:14)

CLEAR STAR OF THE MORNING, O NEW STAR OF JACOB

There are frequent symbolical references in both the Old and the New Testament to stars: "A star shall rise out of Jacob," (Numbers 24:17) ". . . thou shalt rise as the day star" (Job, 11:17). ". . . before the day star I begot thee" (Psalms 109:3). The wise men, seeking the true King, explained: "We have seen his star in the East." (Matthew 2:2). St. Peter, writing to the faithful, assures them: "And we have more firm prophetical word whereunto you do well to attend, as to a light that shineth in a dark place, until the day dawn and the day star arise in your heart." (2 Peter 1:19). In the Apocalypse we read "I am the root and stock of David, the bright and morning star." (Apocalypse 22:16)

VIRGIN MOST WISE

Solomon has much praise of wisdom, especially in the phrases: "The wise shall possess glory; the law of the wise is the fountain of life; a wise woman buildeth her house" (Proverbs, passim). The wisdom of the virgins who took oil in their lamps to be prepared for the Bridegroom's coming is proclaimed in St. Matthew, 25:4. Mary's lamp, ever burning, was kept bright by the oil of her virginity, to welcome the coming of Him who was both her Son and her Bridegroom.

SEVEN FAIR PILLARS AND TABLE DIVINE

Solomon, speaking allegorically of wisdom, says she "hath built herself a house; she hath hewn her out seven pillars. She hath slain her victims, mingled her wine, and set forth her table . . . Forsake childishness, and live, and walk in the ways of prudence." (Proverbs 9:1 and 6)

GATE OF THE SAINTS, PORTAL OF GOD

Jacob, journeying to Mesopotamia in flight from the wrath of Esau and Isaac, had in sleep a vision of angels ascending and descending a ladder. Then the Lord, leaning upon the ladder, promised him that he would be the father of an illustrious people. Jacob on awakening exclaimed: "Indeed, the Lord is in this place, and I knew it not." And trembling, he said: "How terrible is this place! This is no other but the house of God and the gate of heaven." (Genesis 28:16-17)

Throughout the Old Testament, gates and gateways are symbolic of entering into a new life. The royal Psalmist sings: "Open ye to me the gates of justice; I will go in to them, and give praise to the Lord. This is the gate of the Lord: the just shall enter into it." And "Blessed is the man that hath filled his desire with them [children]; he shall not be confounded when he shall speak to his enemies in the gate!" (Psalms 117:19-20, and 126:5)

Our Lord says: "Enter ye in at the narrow gate," and again: "How narrow is the gate and strait the way." (Matthew 7:13,14)

O TERRIBLE AS THE EMBATTLED ARRAY

Addressing the spouse of Christ, Solomon says: "Thou art beautiful, O my love, and sweet and comely as Jerusalem; terrible as an army set in array." (Canticles 6:3)

SOLOMON'S THRONE

"The King also made a great throne of ivory and overlaid it with pure gold; and six steps to go up to the throne . . . There was not such a throne in any kingdom." (2 Par. 9:17-19)

ARK OF THE LAW

The ark of the law is variously mentioned in the Old Testament as the ark of God, the ark of the covenant, the ark of the testimony. In his Epistle to the Hebrews, St. Paul says Noah "framed the ark for the saving of his house" (Hebrews 11:7), and of course there is much mention all through the books of Exodus and Leviticus about the construction of the sacred ark to contain the law given to Moses.

FAIR RAINBOW

"Look upon the rainbow, and bless him that made it; it is very beautiful in its brightness." (Ecclesiasticus 43:12)

"And as the rainbow giving light in the bright clouds, and as the flower of roses in the days of the spring." (Ecclesiasticus 50:8)

"And he that sat was to the sight like the jasper and the sardine stone; and there was a rainbow round about the throne." (Apocalypse 4:3)

AND BUSH WHICH THE PATRIARCH SAW

When Moses received the divine command to rescue his people from Egypt, God called to him in "a flame of fire out of the midst of a bush; and he saw that the bush was on fire and was not burnt." (Exodus 3:2)

GIDEON'S FLEECE

Gideon was one of the first of the Judges of the Old Testament. Seeking a sign from God that he was really chosen to save his people, he prayed: "I will put this fleece of wool on the floor. If there be dew on the fleece only, and it be dry on all the ground beside, I shall know that by my hand, as thou hast said, thou wilt deliver Israel." Though the sign was vouchsafed, he still was not satisfied, and prayed further that on the next trial the fleece alone should be dry, and the dew on all the ground round about. (Judges, 6:37,39)

BLOSSOMING ROD

God confirmed the priesthood of Aaron with the promise: "Whomsoever of these I shall choose, his rod shall blossom." (Numbers 17:5)

SAMSON'S SWEET HONEYCOMB

Samson, on the way to claim his bride from the Philistines, met a young lion that attempted to attack him, but Samson tore him to pieces. Returning some days later, he saw that a swarm of bees had made a honeycomb in the mouth of the dead monster. He ate of the honey and later made the incident an occasion for a riddle: "Out of the eater came forth meat, and out of the strong came forth sweetness." (Judges, 14:14)

Solomon says: "Well-ordered words are as the honeycomb" (Proverbs 16:24), and the Bride in the Canticles: "I have eaten the honeycomb with my honey." (Canticles 5:1)

GARDEN OF PLEASURE

The original scene of our first parents' trial was a paradise of pleasure. *Paradise,* derived from the Greek, means a secluded spot off the beaten track — a park, a grove. Wherever the word is mentioned, the phrase "of pleasure" is added: "The Lord God planted a paradise of pleasure from the beginning . . .," "The Lord God took man and put him into a paradise of pleasure," ". . . and placed before the paradise of pleasure Cherubims . . ." (Genesis 2 and 3 — passim)

CEDAR OF CHASTITY

The wood of the cedar, while soft and malleable, is considered incorruptible. It was one of the woods used in the building of the ark and also of the Temple. The cedars of Libanus were renowned for their strength, grace, and beauty. For the cleansing of leprosy, the High Priests of the Old Law were commanded to dip cedar wood into the blood of a sparrow and sprinkle the leper seven times. (Leviticus 14:7) Cedar trees and cedar wood are mentioned seventy-three times in the Old Testament, sometimes symbolically, at other times factually, but always there is a connotation of strength and purity.

MARTYRDOM'S PALM

The palm in the Old Testament was symbolic of victory. Since the early days of the Church, it has been a sign of the greatest victory of all: the sacrifice of one's life for Christ.

Thou Land Set Apart From Uses Profane

". . . And among the cities which you shall give to the Levites, six shall be separated for refuge." (Numbers 35:6) "Thou shalt separate to thee three cities in the midst of the land." (Deuteronomy 19:2) "Appoint cities of refuge." (Josue 20:2)

David's High Tower

Significant of David's military prowess: wherever he conquered cities, he built at the gate a tower which served the double purpose of vigilance and defense.

Woman Most Valiant

"Who shall find a valiant woman? Far and from the uttermost coasts is the price of her." (Proverbs 31:10)

O Judith Thrice Blest

When Judith returned from her destruction of Holofernes, thereby freeing the Israelites from the Assyrians, "Joachim the High Priest came from Jerusalem to Tethulia with all his ancients to see Judith. And when she was come out to him, they all blessed her, saying: 'Thou art the glory of Jerusalem . . . the honor of our people. For thou hast done manfully, and thy heart hath been strengthened because thou hast loved chastity'." (Judith 15:9-11)

As David Was Nourished in Fair Abishag's Breast

When David the King was very old, no amount of clothing could keep him warm. So they sought through all Israel for a most beautiful maiden who should cherish the king and keep him warm and comfortable by the vigor of her own fair body. (3 Kings 1:1-5)

Saviour of Egypt

Joseph, sold by his brethren into Egypt, won the favor of Pharaoh. By Joseph's wisdom, Egypt was a land of plenty at a time when all the rest of the world was devastated by famine. Because of his plan of conservation, he was hailed as saviour of Egypt. (Genesis 41:33-36) So Holy Mother, become our almoner in this our exile, is able to dispense food of salvation from the treasure houses of the King of Heaven.

Dial of Achaz

Ezechias in his illness was told by Isaias that he would die; by praying to God, he obtained longer life, and in confirmation, received a sign by the sun's turning back. "And Isaias the prophet called upon the Lord; and he brought the shadow ten degrees backward by the lines, by which it had already gone down in the dial of Achaz." (IV Kings 20:11) "And this shall be a sign to thee from the Lord . . . Behold, I will bring again the shadow of the lines, but which it is now gone down in the sun dial of Achaz, with the sun, ten lines backward." (Isaias 38:7,8)

The Serpent's Destroyer

When Satan, in the guise of a serpent, tempted Eve to eat of the forbidden fruit, Almighty God promised: "I will put enmities between thee and the woman, and thy seed and her seed; she shall crush thy head, and thou shalt lie in wait for her heel." (Genesis 3:15)

Lily Among Thorns

"As the lily among thorns, so is my love among the daughters. As the apple tree among the trees of the woods, so is my beloved among the sons. I sat down under his shadow, whom I desire; and his fruit was sweet to my palate!" (Canticles 2:2,3)

❊   ❊   ❊

The foregoing points are not meant, of course, for word-by-word transmission to any-age pupils indiscriminately. They are suggested as a basis of development according to the mental capacity of the class. The conclusion is clear enough:

These praises and prayers I lay at thy feet,
O Virgin of virgins, O Mary most sweet.

Be thou my true guide through this pilgrimage here,
And stand by my side when death draweth near.

X

MAY OR JUNE

Among the feasts that may come either in May or June, Mary, according to the liturgical arrangement, are Pentecost, the feast of the Blessed Virgin Mary as Queen of the Apostles, and the feast of your most Pure Heart.

Pentecost your feast? Oh yes, for you were never separated from your Son in His great feasts, and certainly you would not be apart from the coming of the Holy Ghost on your Son's disciples.

There may have been, Mary, a sudden sense of fear among the others, when that Fiftieth Day the Holy Spirit came. But you — you long had held Him dear, dearly loved and no stranger; for your ear had long been trained to listen for that same intensive force that breathed within the frame of silence; silence which was the setting for your whole life's pattern. The Apostles, your newly bequeathed children, were rejoicing in their gift of tongues; but you, who all these years had kept words in your heart — words — seedling for this hour — you must have knelt mute among the tongues of fire. The Spirit found you as of old adept, pliable, yielding to the whispering of His power.

The gifts and fruits of the Holy Spirit were mirrored forth in the words you did speak, Mary: faith, modesty, chastity in "Whence is this to me — for I know not man." Charity, joy, wisdom in your Magnificat;

patience, long suffering, and meekness in your "Son, why hast thou done so to us?" Charity, goodness, benignity in "They have no wine," and finally wisdom, counsel, and knowledge when you said: "Whatsoever He shall say to you, do ye."

On Saturday, within the octave of Corpus Christi, comes your feast, Mary, as Queen of the Apostles. It is one of those "back of the missal" feasts. Appropriately, the prayer is: "O God, who gavest the Holy Spirit to the Apostles when they were united in prayer with Mary the mother of Jesus, grant to us through the same mother of us as well as Queen of the Apostles that we may be worthy to serve Thy majesty faithfully and to spread abroad the glory of Thy name by word and example." By word and example, Mary — which proceed from the depths of the interior life lived in union with you — that's the "secret weapon" against Communism and against the snares of the devil.

Again, the Saturday *after* the octave of Corpus Christi is celebrated the feast of the Most Pure Heart of Mary. This foreshadows a more recently established feast on August 22 — the feast of your Immaculate Heart. The Epistle for the Mass of your Most Pure Heart is taken from that passionately intense love song, the Canticle of Canticles: "Place me as a seal on thy heart, as a shield on thy arm; for love is strong as death. Many waters cannot quench it, nor the rivers sweep it away. If for love a man should give all his substance, he would despise it as nothing."

This ties in purity not with anemic fears, or scrupulosity, or squeamishness, but with a force very positive and constructive and powerful indeed! O Mother of Beautiful Love, teach love to us!

XI

1. JUNE

This month is not exclusively your Son's month, Mother, for it is seldom that you are far apart from Him. It is the month so eagerly looked forward to: the coming of the summer vacation for the school children who pursued the path of knowledge with more or less willing feet — whatever might be said of the willingness of their minds! The Sisters look forward, too, to the ending of school for another year — sometimes because they are tired and vacation looms nearer, very often because they are looking forward to the annual Retreat; perhaps they too are more or less eagerly anticipating summer school activities.

It is time for teachers to look back upon the year and take stock. How could the lessons have been made more stimulating? How could they have made you better known and loved? Perhaps those Sodality exercises had been too much routine, a practice in discipline, or just so much chattering. That is why, sweet Mother, I prefaced the May-June discussion with a study of your Little Office of the Immaculate Conception, with the avowed purpose of enlivening its recitation.

June is full of feast-day saints who were devoted to you: on the fourth, St. Francis Caracciola. His life illustrates one of the seeming accidents by which you bring it about that souls will to do your Son's will: a letter addressed to another was delivered to him by mistake. It informed him of the founding of a new institute: the Minor Clerks Regular. So he joined, whether the invitation was for him or not (it was meant for another — but what became of that other, Mary?) and gave himself up to the prayer and penance that you have been so insistently asking of the children at LaSalette — Fatima — and still more recently at Beauraing and Banneux.

My mind keeps reverting to all those shrines, O holy Mother, especially in France — over three thousand of them there, at least sixty of which have been declared miraculous in some way or another and have Ecclesiastical approval. Why? Is it because France *needs* you more than any other country? Shrines in Italy, Belgium, Spain, Portugal — all through the South American countries. We — here in the United States — what have we? Nary a vision, or a picture, or a command to have struck a Miraculous Medal of you. Mary darling, I'm not *asking* for these things. I think if there were rumors of you — Mary here, Mary there, I would wait until the Church made official pronouncement, and meanwhile I would companion with you in spirit just as I've been doing all along. But *is* it a compliment that you don't come to us? Is it because you are our Patron, and you are taking care of us just as well without all the paraphernalia of visions with their accompaniment of hysteria, suffering for the privileged ones, disbelief of the hard-hearted, too easy credulity on the part of those seeking novelties? You find the answer for us, Mary, and make us your devoted children under any circumstances.

A Sister who attended summer school at Notre Dame University said that at five-fifteen A.M. (daylight saving time made it even darker) she used to thrill at joining the *crowds* going chapel-ward. It was a concerted movement seemingly without organization. It was just taken for granted that everybody was going to Mass — and at that hour! See? If there are places like this, and devotion like this (and surely Notre Dame is not just one outstanding situation), then we need not feel too neglected if we have no actual apparition, or medal, or miraculous picture to draw crowds to you and to your divine Son.

St. Margaret, honored on the tenth, is one of your children who took you for a model, Mary. As Queen of the Scots, how often she must have saluted you as Queen of angels, of saints, and (in the tumultuous times in which she lived) of *peace*. She was a model of mothers, too, O my blessed Mother, and brought up her eight children in piety, obedience, and love. She was your instrument, sweet Lady of Charity, in her love of the poor and her service toward her neighbor, especially in her care of the orphans.

How you must have loved St. Anthony of Padua, my Mother, for his devotion to the Infant. It must have been yourself who put that Infant in his arms. So characteristic in his tender holding of the Baby that his clients tend to forget that he is a doctor, a confessor, and has written many learned treatises. But we, though we love him, think mostly of the Child in his arms and of his other prerogative: the ability to find lost things. As a matter of record, one little child, on learning the story of the loss of Jesus and the Finding in the Temple said: "Yes, of course — St. Anthony had Him all that time; that's why we pray to him to find lost things."

Five days after St. Anthony's feast, we have St. Ephrem's, the "Harp of the Holy Ghost." O Mother, what delights of inspiration the Holy Spirit poured upon him to enable him to produce his deathless poems about you and the saints. How clever he was, to write these songs as a device for combatting heresies! That's an idea for these times, too, Mary. Please raise up poets who will sing your praises and woo from error those who are wavering or those who have already gone over to the side of evil. But they must produce *good literature* as well as piety!

On the nineteenth, St. Juliana Falconieri joins our June procession, St. Juliana who practiced in a heroic measure the special Servite devotion to your Seven Sorrows. Undoubtedly it was you, my Lady of the Blessed Sacrament, who influenced your Son to communicate the Sacred Host to her miraculously on the day of her death: since she could not eat or drink, she asked that the Host be held near to her heart — whereupon, it entered into her body.

St. Aloysius for the twenty-first, patron of purity, patron of youth, owed his inspiration to you, sweet Mary. It is said that so devoted was he to you that he fell into an ecstasy when he heard any sermon in honor of you. Long ago, when I was still groping toward true devotion to you, Mary, and heard about this, I begged: "Oh, let me hear such sermons!" But the answering thought came: "Perhaps you do hear them — but you haven't enough sense to appreciate their value."

On the second Sunday of June, we have your feast: Our Lady of the Street. The words are prettier, Mary, in Italian: Madonna della Strada. This is a fourteenth century picture of you that has been incorporated in the Gesu church in Rome.

Long ago, on my way home from work, I used to

stop at the Jesuit Church here in our own city, Mary, and kneel at a shrine containing a replica of this picture. I would leave the office at five o'clock, walk up Calvert Street all intent on my own thoughts. Your Shrine, Mary, formed a half-way stop in the long way home, but I never seemed to be in a hurry or specially hungry for dinner. I prayed before your picture for guidance, and finally you showed me the way, O Our Lady of the Way! In you is all the grace of the Way, the Truth, the Light.

The feast on the twenty-fourth — that of the Nativity of St. John Baptist — has definite connection with you, Mary. You were there, assisting Elizabeth, when all the time the Divine Infant was growing in perfection within your womb. It is said that because of John's humble remark: "He must increase, I must decrease," the very arrangement of days conforms, so that from the twenty-fourth on the days decrease in light; whereas from Christmas on, they increase. A poetic detail in the celebration of his feast is the lighting of bonfires on the hilltops, as a symbol of the light appearing to the darkness. O Lady of Light, pray for your children wandering in the darkness of ignorance and perversion!

Another of your miraculous pictures gives us the feast for the twenty-seventh: Our Lady of Perpetual Help. This picture has been confided to the care of the Redemptorists in their Church in Rome. It has been copied and published abroad so faithfully, however, that scarcely anyone is unfamiliar with its background of gold, your ornately-clad figure, your face oh, so sad! The Infant is clinging to you, one sandal dropping off, the angels Michael and Gabriel are presenting to Him the instruments of the passion. For nearly three hundred years, my Mother, graces have been obtained through your intercession under this title: Our Lady of Perpetual Succour!

Father Knox says that Protestants make fun of us because we seem to have so many different "Lady's" — our Lady, health of the sick, our Lady of Knock, our Lady here, there, of this and of that. But he says they don't know the half of it, for each of us has his own private "Lady" to whom he is especially devoted. In fact, many of us have a separate "Lady" for every need: Mary, Queen of Peace in time of strife, Lady of Good Counsel in time of doubt, Refuge of Sinners in time of guilt or temptation or supplication for another's need. But sensible persons know, my Mother, that we are merely satisfying our devotion to you, Mother of God, because above all and through all you are the Mediatress of Graces, and the *Way* to the Truth and the Light. And you will not wonder what manner of salutation is this we make to you, because by now you've had nearly twenty centuries' experience of all manner of salutations!

St. Irenaeus has his day on the twenty-eighth — St. Irenaeus who immortalized his meeting with St. John the Evangelist by the remark: "I have seen him who saw the Lord" — surely a worthy link in the long chain connecting us, even us, with the Apostles and their Master! If he saw him who saw the Lord, he must have been very much impressed with the fact that this beloved disciple was also the one who saw you — who was related to you — who received you from the cross of his dying Lord as his special care.

The next day we come to the feast day, or rather just the commemoration of a very obscure little saint: St. Judith. It is thought that she was the same as

Eadwald, a noble woman of great fame, but of great infamy, too. When, through the grace of God she became a recluse and a penitent, she changed her name to Judith.

There is another Judith of Christian fame — daughter of Charles the Bold who married (against her father's wishes) Baldwin, Count of Flanders. She was the step-mother of Alfred the Great. There is in connection with her a mention of a famous ring — the ring of her espousals, which brings our minds back to your espousals, Mary; and because of you, to the espousals of all Religious — of mine, especially, with the silver ring showing that "I am espoused to Him whom the angels serve, at whose beauty the sun and the moon stand in awe."

The name — Judith — takes us inevitably back to one of your great prototypes in the Old Testament. Her prayer to God for help may well be echoed against the aggressors of today: that the wives and virgins of her people might not be violated: "and know that thou art our God who destroyest wars from the beginning, and the Lord is thy name. Lift up thy arm and crush their power with thy power; let their power fall in their wrath who promised themselves to violate thy sanctuary and defile the dwelling place of thy name. . . . Bring to pass, O Lord, that his [Holofernes'] pride may be cut off with his own sword . . . for this will be a glorious monument for thy name, when he shall fall by the hand of a woman . . . the prayer of humble and meek hath always pleased thee . . . hear me making supplication to thee, presuming on thy mercy . . . and all nations may acknowledge that thou art God and there is no other besides thee."

The praise of her, generously admitted even by

Holofernes and his servants, is certainly still more applicable to you, Mary: "There is not such another woman upon earth in looks, in beauty, and in sense of words." And the praise of the High Priest Joachim, when she returned victorious, is embodied in Masses read in your honor, Mary: "Thou art the glory of Jerusalem, thou art the joy of Israel, thou art the honor of thy people. For thou hast done courageously, and thy heart has been strengthened because thou hast loved chastity."

But — oh, my Mother! there the parallelism ends. Her canticle in its gloating over the defeat of the enemy, is the antithesis of your Magnificat. Only at the end of it may we find an exaltation worthy of you: "Let us sing a hymn to the Lord, let us sing a new hymn to our God. . . . Let thy creatures serve thee, O Adonai, because thou hast spoken and they were made; thou didst send forth thy spirit and they were created and there is no one that can resist thy voice. The mountains shall be moved from the foundations with the waters: the rocks shall melt as wax before thy face. But they that fear thee shall be great with thee in all things."

No, my Mother, I cannot imagine your taking the head of Holofernes and displaying it with such grim assurance, nor offering "for an anathema of oblivion all the arms of Holofernes." Of course, we know that much of this can be applied symbolically, in the same way as your crushing the head of the serpent does not mean you actually stepped on a snake's head. But in this, as in all Sacred Scripture, there is a three-fold application, just as there can be that triple fusion of past, present, and future into the NOW of eternity. The story is essentially historical: there *was* an Assyrian General named Holofernes who filled the Isaelites with fear and trembling, there *was* a dauntless widow, Judith, who circumvented him by trickery and by her beauty. Symbolically we can think of her as your prototype, Mediatress of Graces, overcoming evil, help-ing to procure freedom and peace, O daughter of Israel. Then, as in the history of nations — any nation — so in our own souls the drama is re-enacted. We are ambushed by evil, starved into submission; we need the grace that you will obtain for us, in order to overcome by — trickery? No, not in a bad sense — but to use against the devil his own weapons so that your pure beauty will obtain the victory for us and restore to us the beauty of our souls. O dauntless Mother Mary, pray for us sinners, now — and at the hour of temptation and despair.

2. OUR LADY OF EVERYTHING

Like a hapless poet of not so long ago, I would take my "literary stiletto" and cut out (for special considera-tion) some few of the many titles of Our Lady under which her intercession is invoked in the Litany of Loreto. Unlike him, I cannot hymn her praises in lyric lines, but I can offer a few thoughts on the appropriateness of the titles and of the attributes ascribed to her in the rhythmic recurrence of petitions known as the Litany.

Throughout the centuries, from the very beginning of devotion to Mary, there have been many prayers of responsive petition to her. They were gradually codi-fied and unified into the best known form: the Litany of Loreto, composed mainly during the early years of the sixteenth century, and so called because the invocations took root as a devotion at Loreto in Italy, and were set to music by the choirmaster of the Basilica of Loreto. As needs arose, various titles have been added since.

After the introductory prayers and the invocation to the Holy Trinity usually made at the beginning of any Litany, Mary is asked to pray for us as the Mother of Christ, of our Saviour, of divine grace, and of good counsel. She is called a mother most pure, most chaste, undefiled, and admirable.

Such adjectives we traditionally use in praise of Mary. It is easily seen, too, how in recognition of her virginity we would use the appellations: prudent, venerable, renowned, powerful, merciful, and faithful. Most fittingly and naturally also we salute her as a queen — Queen of angels with whom even during her mortal life she held communication, of Patriarchs who sighed for the coming of her Son, or of Prophets who foretold His coming; of Apostles whom her Son selected and to whom He confided the care of her after His death; of martyrs, of confessors, of virgins, of all saints, and of the most holy Rosary.

In the midst of these easily understandable titles, however, we suddenly come upon what seems a flowering forth of poetic imagery, a veritable mosaic of oriental fantasy. Our Lady is hailed as a mirror of justice, a seat of wisdom, a spiritual vessel of honor and of devotion, a mystical rose, a tower of David and of ivory, a house of gold, the ark of the covenant, gate of heaven, and morning star.

Let us examine into the meaning of these salutations: *Mirror of Justice:* In ancient times, a mirror was merely a polished sheet of metal. It was called a "speculum" and of course it fulfilled then the same purpose as now: something to be looked into, something that is made to reflect an image. We can look into the shining soul of Mary to see her justice, which reflects the Sun of Justice most faithfully. Mirrors are frequently used to catch the light of the sun and direct its rays to a dark corner. Like wisdom, Mary can be called the unspotted mirror of God's majesty.

Seat of Wisdom: the word "seat" is used to connote a site, abode, residence, or location. We find frequent mention in the Scriptures of a judgment seat, a mercy seat, seat of iniquity, of honor. Mary herself sings in her *Magnificat:* "He has cast down the mighty from their seat." In her, happily, resides wisdom as in its rightful abode and place of honor.

Spiritual Vessel, Vessel of Honor, Vessel of Singular Devotion: here again the scriptural writers use the word "vessel" as a person in whom trust is reposed, or in whom resides some specific quality. St. Paul says we have the treasure of grace in earthen vessels. He also mentions vessels of honor and of dishonor. Christ, in speaking of St. Paul, called him a vessel of election. Jeremias uses the term reproachfully in calling Jechonias (one of the unworthy descendants of David who finally betrayed Israel into the hands of the Babylonians) an earthen vessel and a broken vessel. Again, speaking through the mouth of Jeremias about the enemies of Judah, God says: "I have broken Moab as a useless vessel." In contrast, the Handmaid of the Lord is saluted as a truly spiritual vessel, one of honor, and one in whom the virtue of devotion, or filial piety, found worthy habitation.

Mystical Rose: Flowers have always been associated with our Lady. Mary, like Wisdom, could sing: "I was exalted like a palm tree in Cades, and as a rose plant in Jericho." She may claim as directed to herself the command of God: "Hear me, ye divine offspring, and bud forth as the rose planted by the brooks of waters." She responds: "I took root in an honorable people." Recently, very recently, she sent forth a shower of roses as proof to the people that she wished her message of Fatima to be heard and heeded. One of her petals, examined in the chemical laboratory, was found to be impervious to all tests — it was made of no substance known to scientists. Though this miracle has not been pronounced upon by the Church, we can still exclaim: Mystical — and mysterious — rose indeed!

The next two invocations compare her to a tower: David's tower, and tower of ivory. Now, a tower has a three-fold significance. It is high, placed above the surrounding buildings so that the dwellers therein could survey the country with unimpeded view; it is a place of advantage for defense; and it is also a place of seclusion and privacy, so that the inhabitants thereof have a distinction not shared with those not admitted to the tower. Height for clearer view of the world, defense against the invasion of evil, and the unique privilege of sinlessness are Mary's prerogatives.

Consider, too, the qualities of ivory. Ivory has always been esteemed for its beauty and value. It is dense substance, with pores close and compact, filled with a gelatinous solution which not only contributes a beautiful polish, but also makes it easy to work with. Unlike bone, ivory requires no special preparation. In its natural state, it is fit for immediate working.

Thus our Lady, because of her Immaculate Conception, was already uniquely and fittingly prepared to fulfill her great role. Ivory has always been remarkably sensitive to sudden extremes of temperature; and our Lady, too, is responsive to the depths of misery or to the heights of joy, purity, and zeal. Furthermore, in the valuable product of ivory, nothing is wasted — even the dust is used for polishing, and also for preparing ink. So with Mary: her smallest act or thought or word must have caused God all but infinite satisfaction, and must have formed a medium whereby the Holy Spirit could write His message to the minds of men.

House of Gold: the word "house" is used here in the same significance as tower and seat. Like ivory, gold is esteemed by mankind because of its qualities: it is brilliant, unalterable, permanent in air or water, and under all conditions of weather. Likewise are brilliance, stability, and great value the qualities of our Lady who chants exultantly about her "house of gold" as she sings: "In the holy dwelling place I have ministered before him."

Ark of the Covenant: It would seem that no plan of God in the Old Testament was worked out in more meticulous detail than the Ark or little house which contained vessels for sacrifice, an altar for incense, the loaves of bread, and the tablets on which were engraved the Law given to Moses. But the incense, the bread, and the stern commands were all figures of the Old Law which were to give place to a New Dispensation, promulgated in mercy. Fittingly, then, do we call her whose pure body furnished the "Blood of the New Testament" a new Ark, a sacred deposit for the Holy of Holies. The first Ark of the Covenant accompanied the people in all their wanderings, until finally Solomon housed it magnificently in the first Temple

of Jerusalem. Likewise, the Ark of the Covenant of
the New Dispensation sings: "And my abode is in the
full assembly of the saints."

Gate of Heaven: Gates by their very nature are
meant either to shut in something very precious and
worthy of being guarded, or else to lead to something
that is desirable of attainment. Unlike doors, however,
they do not form a solid barrier; most gates allow
visibility for the precious thing they guard, or the
desirable object upon which they open. There were
many gates in Solomon's Temple, variously described
as the east gate, fish gate, the gate of the fountain,
gate of the valley, flock gate, water gate, judgment
gate, watch gate, earthen gate — and finally St. Luke
in the Acts of the Apostles mentions the Beautiful
Gate. Many of these gates can typify Mary. She is
the East Gate through which the Hope of the Orient
has passed. From this valley of tears it is she who
allows us to look toward the most desirable of all goals
— Heaven. Fish, fountains, flocks, water, earth in its
fertility all have qualities that reside in her, for she is
the fountain of graces, and a shepherdess of the flock.
And when the Gates of Heaven swing open to each
individual soul that is redeemed, it will be because of
her, the channel of all graces.

Morning Star: What rich, deep connotation the
stars have, in all the imagery of the inspired Books!
Baruch writes: "The stars have given light in their
watches and rejoiced; they were called, and they said
Here we are, and with cheerfulness they have shined
forth to him that made them." Mary's "Behold the
handmaid of the Lord" is her equivalent of *Here we
are* as she radiated forth to Him her humility and her
willingness. Balaam, unworthy prophet though he

was, proclaimed truly: "A star shall rise out of Jacob;" the Psalmist sings: "In the brightness of the saints, from the womb before the day star I begot thee." St. Peter promises a day star that shall rise in our hearts, and St. John in the Apocalypse, reporting the words of Jesus, writes: "I am the root and stock of David, the bright and morning star." Hence many a watcher through a night of despair has looked for the first visible sign of the dawn: the morning star, which should assure new hope in the coming of a tranquil day.

The conclusion? All beautiful things are comparable to Mary. Oh, Cause of our joy! Cause of our joy in stars, roses, ivory, gold, all lovely and useful and graceful and poetic things, pray for us!

XII

1. JULY

Early in the month dedicated to your Son's Precious Blood comes the feast of your Visitation. At the time, your own pure blood was forming within you the Body and Blood that He gave to the world — to sinners — to me.

You are Our Lady of Visits, my Mother: your first one — Elizabeth looked out across the hills and saw a little girl, hastening, quick to serve. There have been many visits since: as you grew older, older (but young with that mystical fusion of time with eternity), your visits came to younger ones: to Bernadette, Melanie, Maximin, to Juan Diego of Guadalupe. O Mary, keep us young in heart, keep us atuned to your message when you come. And please let us recognize you, though whence is this to us that the Mother of our Lord should visit us?

Your third word, sweet Mother, was that greeting to Elizabeth. We are not told what you said. The greetings of today are very informal, reduced mostly to a sort of explosive "Hi!" but we may be sure that yours, while stately in grace, consonant with the custom and good manners of the time, deferential to the aged Elizabeth, was also sweetly simple and unassuming. Whatever were the actual words, they were powerful enough to enlighten Elizabeth and make her realize two things: one the towering strength of your faith (blessed art thou that thou hast *believed*), the second the divine secret of your pregnancy (whence is this to me that the Mother of my Lord should come to me).

It is good to think that on our visits to the poor, the sick, and the ignorant, the Mother of our Lord comes with us. We call these calls "visitations." They may be only to our own families, relatives, friends, or families of our pupils where there is death, sickness, or sorrow. In this case our family re-union brings consolation to both the Religious and the family. It may be we are privileged to go on a *real* visitation such as our Foundress conducted in Ireland, where we can take food, clothing, medicine; where we can minister to a patient who cannot get supplies to fill his basic needs even in these days of organized social service and welfare. In such poor homes, while cleaning, cooking, ministering, we can preach and instruct, either by good example or by actual speech. My blessed Mother of Mercy, Lady of Visits, I thank you for these privileges!

The fifth of July is devoted to one of your loving sons who added your name to his own: St. Anthony Mary Zaccharia. He should be one that teachers could appeal to for intercession, especially as the Gradual for his Mass quotes the burning words of St. Paul: "For God is my witness how I long after you in the bowels of Jesus Christ. And this I pray: that your charity may more and more abound in knowledge and all understanding; that you may approve the better things, that you may be sincere and without offense unto the day of Jesus Christ."

What better words could we address to our pupils? We do indeed long after their good in the heart of Jesus, that they may abound in the knowledge we can offer them. But understanding must come from the Holy Spirit, Mary my Mother. Certainly we pray that they may "approve the better things" (so much depends on their approval in the sense of getting their cooperation). Assuredly do we want them to be "without offense."

We'll pass over eleven days, Mother, and come to a very special day for you and for us. Special for us not only because it is your feast, but also it was the feast of our Mother M. Carmelita. Her simple, child-like devotion to you was a counterpart of her being (also like you) a "valiant woman — she has considered a field and bought it" for she was a woman of business and outstanding genius for organization and government. Yet mercy and motherliness were never found lacking in her. She was as approachable for those asking for some little thing like a remedy for a head-ache, as for a contractor coming to discuss with her plans for building. O Mary! if she is not already united with you in Heaven, entreat your sweet Son to grant her rest and peace and light soon — soon. How could it be otherwise, considering her great devotion to you, and her great zeal for the interests of your Son?

It is the feast of another of your apparitions, Mother. You came to St. Simon Stock and promised special blessings to all who wore the habit of his order; and this "scapular promise" has been mercifully extended to all your devoted children. "Be mindful, O virgin Mother, to speak good things before God's face in our behalf, so that He may turn away His anger from us."

Your feast, Our Lady of Mount Carmel, is celebrated by a special procession at the Catholic University. All over the campus, students and teachers march in honor of you, while anxious young Carmelites act as ushers and guides and leaders in saying your Rosary. They

are pretty good shepherds for your children, my
Mother; bless their work of retreats and preaching
and most of all the cultivation of that "interior life"
which is to form the lever that will lift the world.

We cannot very well overlook the twenty-second,
feast of Mary Magdalen the penitent, who performed
for Jesus the Man the lovely services you performed
for Him as a Baby: anointing His feet, His hair; who
shared with you a place beneath His cross and who
(according to the Scriptural record — though we know
you must have been the first to see Him, Mother) was
the first to greet Him at His Resurrection. The contrast between you, Virgin most pure, and the repentant
sinner who had been forgiven much because of her
great love is the sort of thing that Divine Mercy loves
to bring about, "for love is strong as death, the lamps
thereof are lamps of fire and flames." And the inter-
vening clause that I have omitted: "jealousy is hard
as hell," shows that this love is not a namby-pamby
thing of sentiment!

Three days later, we have feasts for your two sons,
Mary: the first a relative of yours, St. James, Bishop
of Jerusalem, who had a very ambitious mother;
imagine! asking for the best places for her sons. You
did not have to make a plea to the Eternal Father,
Mary. You did not have to say: "Grant that this my
Son Jesus may sit at Thy right hand, O God my
Father," for that had already been assured to you by
Gabriel. You were not asking, either, for any special
place for yourself; but still, like your Son, you had
tolerance for those who (before their enlightenment
by the Holy Spirit) were obfuscated by earth-bound
dreams of glory and prestige. St. James did indeed
occupy the place that Jesus and His Father had des-

tined for him, and his importance consists not only in his position at Jerusalem, but also in his tomb in Spain, the shrine of Compostella (field of the star) where so many graces and miraculous cures have been wrought.

O Lady of the Star, star of the field as well as of the sea, pray for your children, whether their places be lowly or high!

That other son of yours celebrated on the twenty-fifth is one whose name places you very close to him: Christ-bearer, for you are the Christ-bearer in very truth, my Mother. St. Christopher is a patron of travellers; but no saint really abrogates any prerogative of yours; all their qualities and traits and special predilections lead us back to you — and you lead us to Jesus.

Our Lady of the Way, protector of travellers, pray for the wanderers, give them safe conduct!

The next day we come to the celebration of your own mother's feast. So little we know of her actually, Mary, but so much do we experience the power of her intercession, judging from her shrine at Beaupré. Here again, any thought of her leads us immediately to you: "Good Saint Ann, mother of her who is our life, our sweetness, and our hope, pray to her for us and obtain our request."

On the twenty-ninth, we honor St. Martha — dear Martha who because of a mistaken interpretation of our Lord's reply to her is not always given the reverence she deserves. You must have loved her, Mary, for like you she was a good housekeeper, and she gave your Son hospitality at a time when those who sheltered Him risked the displeasure, even the violent persecution of Scribes, Pharisees, Priests who were hounding Him, drawing snares about Him closer and closer, so as to apprehend Him at last.

Perhaps it was Martha, Mary, who gave you the veil which was afterwards donated to Charlemagne by the Empress Irene (how did *she* get it?). Charlemagne brought it to France, and much later, in 876 it was offered to Chartres by Charles the Bald. It must have been exquisite indeed, woven as it was of the purest and finest silk thread, about six yards long — such a veil as only a rather wealthy person could afford. Or was it (the imagination loves to play around with it!) an heirloom, handed down from St. Ann, going back further in antiquity to Ruth, to Esther, or to Judith? Was it the veil you wore on Calvary, Mother, its long folds shrouding your grief-bowed figure?

The fourth Saturday before the fourth Sunday of July comes another "M.P.A.L." feast — that of the Blessed Virgin, Mother of Mercy. It is a forerunner of our feast on the twenty-fourth of September. The Collect is particularly redolent of your characteristic, O Mother of the merciful God: "O God, whose mercy is without number, grant us through the intercession of the Mother of Thy only-begotten Son, that we may deserve to experience this mercy, spread so widely abroad on this earth, and thus come to your glory in heaven" (and to your Mother's glory, O Father of Mercies)!

"Through the intercession of Mary" — these words or their equivalent occur so often in the prayers at various Masses. Mary, you are indeed the gateway to God, so that we may pray in the words of Psalm 23: "Lift up, O Gates, your lintels; reach up ye ancient portals, that the King of glory may enter in."

And when we have attained the fulfillment of all our prayers, we can echo with satisfaction and ever greater triumph the words of Psalm 121: "And now we have set foot within thy gates, O Jerusalem." — heavenly Jerusalem, we enter our Mansion of eternal delights through Mary and with Mary.

GATEWAY TO GOD

2. GATEWAY TO GOD

"Through Mary to Christ.   Through Christ's sacred manhood to the Holy Ghost.   Through the Holy Ghost we go to the Holy Trinity.   Absorbed in the Divine One-in-Three . . ."

This I quoted, inaccurately but exuberantly, from Garrigou-Lagrange's *The Three Ages of the Interior Life.*   As he, in turn, had gotten the doctrine from St. Thomas, I felt the idea was worth repeating, no matter in whose words it was clothed.

My friend didn't let me finish.   She was an earnest seeker, but was deeply tainted (and *tainted* is a tragic word here) with a mixture of Godless intellectualism, Lutheran rebellion, and Pelagian heresy.   She had her objection:

"All those media!   I prefer to go to God direct."

"But how?" I asked.   "And do you?   God is a pure spirit . . ."

"And my soul is a spirit."

"But your soul, in this life, is united to your body. Until death it needs your body for its very existence. And as long as you are a human being, you are composed of body and soul, each component needing the other. God, it seems, has built the whole fact of existence upon indirection.   The earth produces grass and plants to nourish animals and us; the animals nourish us also . . ."

"But how materialistic you are!   God is a spirit and must be worshiped in the spirit."

"As long as we're not pure spirits, we can't separate the body from this worship.   I'm not being materialistic in a derogative sense, I'm merely facing material facts when I recognize the necessity of media.   It's the same in the life of the mind: we gain knowledge through our senses, through the use of books and objects around us. We bring the ability and the achievements of the senses to bear on the things of the spirit . . ."

I wasn't convincing her. No argument would ever substitute for a humble acceptance of truth received in a spirit of faith. But I used her remark as a springboard for my own reflections:

As long as we are on this earth and continue to grow and develop in a normal way, we will never be independent of different sorts of mediation. In spite of new developments in food products and food processes, we still need the good earth to bring forth fruits and plants. We still need to take food for the sustenance, repair, and strengthening of our bodies. We still need exterior objects to feed, exercise, and develop the senses. We will continue to need our senses to furnish knowledge to our minds. And we still need knowledge to attain to the dignity of understanding and wisdom.

Likewise, no matter how high in sanctity we may become, we shall still, while on this earth, need Christ in the Blessed Sacrament, we shall still, thank God, need Mary in her role of mediatrix.

We do not surrender our integrity by acknowledging our need of media. Rather, we acknowledge our privilege and honor of exercising free will and rationality by making use of the media with discrimination and good judgment until we arrive (ah, happy consummation!) at a state beyond free will: the perfect liberty of the children of God.

Meanwhile, we do not scorn the book that gives us the knowledge we seek. We are not ashamed to go to a teacher who has the skill and learning we ourselves would acquire. We do not disdain the bridge that leads us across a torrent and enables us to continue our journey.

If, after wandering in desert, swamp, or dark forest, we come to a pathway; and that pathway leads to a wall, we know the wall must have been erected to guard something precious, secluded — something that must be kept secure. But we know, too, that according to the usage of walls and barriers and divisions, there must also be a gateway; and the gateway furnishes entrance for those privileged to share the seclusion of whatever precious security the wall is meant to guard.

All this reasoning in figures of speech would probably not convince my friend. But it does produce within my spirit a delight and refreshment in the consideration that Mary is the gateway; Mary is the entrance to peace and security; but also the entrance to a state far more dynamic and active than the mere passivity of peace and security. She is the gateway to joy, love, and beauty.

How good of God to give us such a gateway! The gateway to goodness, grace, Truth, and Wisdom is herself good, full of grace, true, and wise. In the Liturgy, all lovely, poetic description of abstract wisdom is applied concretely to Mary. The passionately intense description of love in the Canticle of Canticles is made to serve as her Epistle on the feast of the Most Pure Heart of Mary.[1]

"Place me as a seal over thy heart . . . for love is strong as death . . . many waters cannot quench charity

---

[1] This Mass is celebrated in some localities the Saturday after the Octave of Corpus Christi.

. . . a man will give all his substance for love, and having gained love, he'd despise the ruinously sacrificial price as though it were nothing."

Truly, it were worth traversing swamp, desert, and dark forest if such labors be the price of attaining to a gateway leading to perfect love.

From a little child plucking daisies for Mary's May altar and reciting his "Holy Mary, Mother of God," to the ineffable dignity of St. Bernard with his "O clement, O loving, O sweet Virgin Mary"; from the most wretched of sinners who cries "Pray for me now, and at the hour of my death," to the exquisitely pure and powerful Gabriel, who sweeps about her in Heaven, repeating lyrically his "Hail, full of grace," — all seek her, all rejoice in her, all salute her:

"Gateway to God, lead us to Him!"

But when we have attained our goal, when we can turn and see the long way we have traversed, we can yet rejoice that while Mary is truly the way to Truth and Light, not even at the summit and center of holiness do we leave her behind us. She is with us still, presenting us to Him:

Through Mary to Christ; through His sacred Humanity to the Holy Spirit; through the Holy Spirit to union with God the Father in power, God the Son in love, God the Holy Spirit in wisdom.

3. THE IMMACULATE HEART OF MARY

We are having more frequent opportunities to honor Mary in these days which may indeed be days of turmoil, terror, and uncertainty; but in union with her, and trusting in her, they may also be days of inner peace and confidence.

There is a comparatively new feast instituted in her

honor: that of the Immaculate Heart of Mary for the twenty-second of August. In the Mass of this feast, the first part of the Introit urges us to come with confidence to the throne of grace, that we may obtain mercy and may find opportune help; while the second part is Mary's answer, assuring us:

"My heart hath uttered a good word, I speak my works (words of mercy) to the King."

In the Epistle she tells us: "I am the mother of fair love, and fear, and knowledge, and of holy hope. In me is all hope of life and goodness. Come over to me all you that desire me, and be filled with my superabundance."

The Gospel tells the story of our heritage — the bequeathing of Mary to us from the Cross. The Post Communion prays that we who venerate her might experience the intercession of her Immaculate Heart, so that we may be freed from present dangers and may attain to eternal joys. The whole Mass forms a unified thesis on the attributes of Mary's heart.

Still more recently than the August 22nd feast has come the dedication of the First Saturday of the month to her Immaculate Heart — a day to be celebrated by meditation on the mysteries of her Rosary, and by close attention to our duties offered up as penance in honor of her.

Now — why *heart?* Why does the Church propose for our devotion and veneration, first the Sacred Heart of Jesus, and then the Immaculate Heart of Mary?

Why not foot — the feet of Jesus which are declared blessed because they traveled over hills and valleys, bringing the good tidings of redemption? And the feet of Mary that went about, whether hastening over the hills to help Elizabeth, trudging back and forth to the Temple, to Egypt, or merely walking about the

earthen floor of her home when she went about her
tasks of sweeping, cooking, and washing? Or shoulder
— the shoulder of Christ that carried the Cross, the
shoulder of Mary on which the Infant Jesus rested?
Or head — Christ's head crowned with thorns, Mary's
head with its amber-gold hair that the playful hands of
the Baby Jesus must have fondled?

In the Canticle of Canticles, every part of the body
of the Beloved is described, praised, and proposed for
admiration. But in the devotion which the Church
now offers, it is the heart alone which is singled out
for love and praise: Christ's Sacred Heart, Mary's
Immaculate Heart.

Not the mind? No, though speaking in a merely
human sense, we may consider the mind of Mary surely
worthy of hyperdulia; and we may yet be favored with
a feast of the mind of Mary. It is the mind of a poet
and orator, as proved by the Magnificat. It is a lawyer-
like mind, keenly capable of asking questions that go
direct to the crux of the matter:

"How can this be done?" or "Why hast Thou done
so to us?" It is the mind of an organizer and ad-
ministrator that could reach a momentous decision
promptly and announce it firmly:

"Be it done unto me according to thy word."

"Whatsoever He shall say to you, do!"

But neither is it her soul that is proposed as reason
for a special feast. Her soul was the direct recipient
of the gift of immaculateness; the privilege pertained
mainly to her soul — that of no guilt from Adam or
from the waywardness of individual weakness.

So, why the heart? Because the heart is recognized
as the seat of the emotions, the citadel of the affec-
tions, the fountain-head of motives. By synecdoche,
the heart is made to stand for the sum total of char-

acteristics that go to make up a person. We speak of a fickle heart, or a faint heart; the heart is called hard, wicked, fond, pure, candid, blighted, or true — according to the dominating trait of the individual which determines his personality. But the heart is also a catalyst in relation to exterior events or circumstances or the impact of other personalities and the interior reaction thereto.

Confucius proclaims this truth: "The heart of the wise, like a mirror, should reflect all objects without being sullied by any." (And Mary is the mirror of justice.)

Lord Chesterfield says: "The heart has such an influence over the understanding that it is worthwhile to engage it in our interest. All women are guided by nothing else [!] and it has so much to say even with men — and the ablest men, too — that it commonly triumphs in every struggle with the understanding."

Gerald Massey's figurative description, while meant to bring out the pivotal point of *Wedded Love,* may well be applied to Mary:

"The heart is like an instrument whose strings
  Steal nobler music from life's many frets.
  The golden threads are spun through suffering's
    fire,
  Wherewith the marriage robes in heaven are
    woven,
  And all the rarest hues of human life
  Take radiance and are rainbowed out in tears."

Of Mary, more than of any other creature, it could be said that she never fretted after the round pegs and the square pegs of human affairs, for she realized that only the Triune God could fit and fill her triangular heart. Yet by the very reason that it was filled and flooded with the Divinity, it overflowed to mankind with the divine attributes of pity and love and charity and service. Truly hers is the *wise heart that reflects all objects without being sullied by any.* But hers is also the powerful catalyst that transforms the ugliness of woe, pain, and conflict into the *rarest hues of human life,* which through devotion to her *take radiance* and *rainbow out,* even though *in tears.*

This is shown so clearly in the history of her various apparitions at Lourdes, Fatima, Guadalupe, and countless other places which have blossomed forth in miracles of healing. It is shown even more clearly by her non-appearances; that is, by her giving evidence of care, compassion, and influence in a spiritual way, without any outward appeal to the senses. For, while there may possibly be some country that cannot boast of a shrine of Mary dedicated because of her apparition to some favored soul, there cannot surely be any country, location, sea, or land, where Mary's name has not been invoked with the subsequent experience of her graciousness.

Mankind has come to a deep heart when it has appealed to Mary — a heart whose depths have never yet been plumbed. But if our hearts are right with her heart, we may hope to scale the heights; for Robert Ingersoll may proclaim hopelessly: "Life is a narrow vale between the cold and barren peaks of two eternities. We strive in vain to look beyond the heights," but, enlightened by Mary's wisdom, we can exult that "the everlasting heights are given to us for our inheritance."

XIII

AUGUST

From September until August! Arbitrarily perhaps, but liturgically, the Church has thus traced the cycle of your life. Seemingly, Mary, you hastened the "hour" of your Son (and therefore His separation from you) by your plea: "They have no wine." Perhaps by your flaming love you hastened the hour of your coming to Him, which we celebrate this month — your Dormition, your Assumption.

Hour? We might assume, Mary, that the significant hours of your life were: that of Gabriel's announcement to you, that of your Son's death, then of His appearance to you; and lastly that of your falling asleep — to open your eyes upon the glorious welcome of angels, saints, and the Holy Trinity.

For ourselves, none of us truly knows or can say with authority: "This is the loveliest hour, this is the saddest. This is the most important hour — that the most insignificant." Certainly we do not remember the first hour of our life of grace, and just as certainly we won't be able to say: "This is the last — this is the last hour of my life." But if all our hours, all our days and months and years are gathered up in you, Mary, then they are all great, and grace-filled, and significant. Like you, we can then share in the exquisite symphony of utter giving — that we may experience the unbearable sweetness of utter receiving back from the hands of our all-giving God.

It is fitting that your Assumption should come in the
middle of the month: thus all your feasts for the first
fourteen days lead up to it, and those that follow are
"trailing clouds of glory" in reflecting its brilliance.
Joining the long procession of your privileged ones,
St. Alphonsus is honored on the second. St. Alphonsus,
who added your name to his own, who founded the
Redemptorists to glorify your Son's mercy, and who
wrote for you "The Glories of Mary." It is said that
his book is such an all-comprehensive treatise that he
must have read all that was ever written about you,
Mary, up to his time. Humbly I cannot but realize
how absorbing must have been both his research and
his writing!

On the fourth comes St. Dominic, that hound of
God to whom you gave the Rosary in order that he
might by this method of prayer combat the Albigensian
heresy rampant during his time. This day, heavenly
Mother, is the anniversary of my own sweet mother's
death — Mary Regina — who was surely not the least
of your devoted clients.

The next day comes what I like to call one of your
whimsical feasts: such a mixture of human endeavor
with divine inspiration and revelation! St. Mary Major
— our Lady of the Snows (nice of you to let this feast
come in what is usually the most torrid of weather!).
You covered with snow, my Mother, the exact location,
area, and shape of the piece of ground where you
wanted your church built. Later — at Walsingham —
you were to reverse this particular manifestation of
your will, and cover with dew all BUT the desired location of your shrine. You got these ideas from that
mighty warrior, Gideon, with his fleece.[1] And that

---

[1] Judges, 6: 37 and 39.

fleece-sign, Mother, has been applied to you in a mystical sense, too.

In the church of St. Mary Major which was thus built according to your snow-given dimensions, we have treasures comparable to those at Chartres: the manger in which you laid your Son at Bethlehem; and here too is found the picture that St. Luke the Evangelist painted of you. O Mother, what riches!

On the thirteenth, coming so appropriately near to your final great feast, we hail you Refuge of Sinners. Your body was taken from us, Mary, but you are still our refuge in this vale of tears, this vale of tears that becomes most becomingly joyful and exultant because of the many graces you have mediated for us.

Then your great day: the new Mass for you on that feast gives adulation to you: "A great sign appeared in heaven — a woman clothed with the sun, and the moon under her feet; and on her head a crown of twelve stars." I like the Introit of the older Mass, too, which is used for so many of your feasts: "Let us rejoice, celebrating a feast in honor of the Blessed Virgin Mary, at whose Assumption the angels rejoice and praise the Son of God." Then are added the inspired words of Psalm 44 which you must have said in your heart so many times: "My heart has uttered a good word. I speak my works to the King."

The Collect of your new Mass, Mary, begs that, intent on higher things, we may deserve to be partakers of your glory. That is particularly timely now when materialistic considerations, economic and political problems, wars and rumors of war tie our poor hearts to earth.

The next day we celebrate the feast of St. Joachim, your father, the husband of St. Ann — a double feast made so because your Son's Vicar, Leo XIII was devoted to his name-saint.

We must not overlook the twentieth, the feast of St. Bernard, who composed our beloved prayer: "Remember, O most pious virgin Mary that never was it known that anyone who fled to thy protection, implored thy help, or sought thy intercession was left unaided." *Never was it known!* St. Bernard said that, Mary and you have never disproved it.

All this week we are harking back to the glory of your Assumption; and on the octave we have the joyous new feast of your Immaculate Heart. I have prefaced this August discussion with a study of that Mass, Mary, but oddly I omitted recognition of your lovely Collect praying that Almighty God who prepared a dwelling worthy of the Holy Spirit would grant us the grace to *live* according to His heart, which was mirrored so faithfully in your heart, my Mother Mary.

Your body has been taken from us, Mary. It was not subject to the horrible mutilation wrought upon so many of your martyrs, O Queen of martyrs; for example, your own relative St. John whose beheading is commemorated on the twenty-ninth. Whatever sorrow or anguish you endured for our sakes, you never defaced that holy body of yours as did, for example, St. Rose of Lima — though I'm sure the penance she practiced must have been inspired by the Holy Spirit and pleasing to your Son.

As though to console us for your going away, the Saturday after the feast of St. Augustine comes your feast: Lady of Consolation, when we pray: "O Lord Jesus Christ, Father of mercies and God of all consolation, grant us that as we rejoice in the title of your

most holy Mother, Our Lady of Consolation, so we
may merit to arrive at companionship with her in
heaven."

You have left us. You must have been about sixty-
three years old, Mary, when you expired with love
and the Angels came for you. I want to think, Mary,
that like the body of your Son your own was extra-
ordinarily healthy, strong, vigorous — Yet, fittingly, the
last feast we come to before we re-begin the cycle
with your birth, we celebrate you as "Health of the
Sick" — that's the Saturday before the last Sunday in
August. In all your apparitions, you have shown your
solicitude for the sick. Cures have followed your
footsteps, healing waters have sprung forth. Cures
have both preceded and followed the devotion of your
children at many of your shrines.

Sickness, Mary, has brought many great graces (all
the more extraordinary in that Thomas à Kempis only
too truly writes: "Few are improved by sickness"),
but it would be morbid to consider that in itself sickness is of merit. That is why the Collect for this Mass
makes us pray with confidence:

"Grant we beseech Thee, O Lord God, that Thy
servants may rejoice in perennial health of mind and
body, and through the intercession of the glorious
Virgin Thy Mother, we may be freed from all sorrow
and come to the enjoyment of everlasting gladness."

My Mother Mary, I have roamed the year with you.
I have traversed the universe with you, I have glimpsed
the marvels of the spiritual world. Besides the miracles of grace, I have seen flowers, springs of water,
shrines, mighty buildings and institutions rise into
existence at your wish and under your inspiration.

Everywhere, Mother, there are traces of you. You are at home in the depths of degradation that you may raise up souls for your Son. You are above and beyond all the pinnacles of sanctity that may be claimed for all the Saints. The Journal is finished but not ended; for we can but begin the cycle again on a different plane, from a different aspect.

May this sketchy three-fold record of me, my heredity, environment, influence, and circumstances bring me to the delights of the painless, puzzle-less, all-embracing Love of eternal life, where I shall solve the equation of *your* three tenses, plus those elements that went to the making of you. Please greet me in the lovely NOW of eternity, and lead me to Jesus.

Our Lady of "now," Our Lady of Everything, pray for us.